ENCHANTING THE WORLD

The Vision of Twentieth-Century Catholic Writers

James and
Evelyn Eaton Whitehead

A Crossroad Book
The Crossroad Publishing Company
New York

The Crossroad Publishing Company
www. CrossroadPublishing.com
© 2018 by James and Evelyn Whitehead

Cover design by George Foster
Library of Congress Cataloging-in-Publication Data available from the Library of Congress.

ISBN 978-0-8245-9906-5

DEDICATION

For Bernard Lee, S.M.

The world is charged with the grandeur of God.
It will flame out like shining from shook foil.

—Gerard Manley Hopkins

As Catholics, we find our houses and our world haunted by
a sense that the objects, events, and persons of daily life are
revelations of grace.

—Andrew Greeley, *The Catholic Imagination*

Contents

Prologue:
A God-Haunted World

ℭ℞

"The Catholic imagination . . . views the world and all that is in it as enchanted, haunted by the Holy Spirit and the presence of grace."

—Andrew Greeley, *The Catholic Imagination*

We emerge from a production of *The Lion King* exclaiming, "That was magical." A review praises "the bewitching theatrical spell cast" by a particular play. Catholic novelist Evelyn Waugh, in *Brideshead Revisited*, portrays a young man anticipating romance as entering "that low door in the wall . . . which opened on an enclosed and enchanted garden."[1]

Art and literature are in the business of enchantment. Sculptures, sonatas, paintings, novels conjure creations meant to captivate and charm. Art lures us with delights we cannot fully name. We return again and again to paintings that absorb our attention, not even knowing what it is that so demands our presence. A mother reads her daughter a fairy tale, and the child insists, "Read it again." She is not finished with it. As love blooms between two persons, they talk and talk some more; they cannot finish the conversation. All these are signals of enchantment. For the religiously inclined, these are also signals of transcendence.

The story we will tell concerns the efforts of Catholic authors in the twentieth century to describe a world that is both disenchanted and yet teeming with haunting clues about the presence of God and the miracle of grace. These writers turned to metaphors of nature—the charm of a garden and the setting of the sun—to signal both enchantment and a world darkened by its loss. And they turn to the *second language* of religious images—Ash Wednesday, Holy Week, a chapel's sanctuary lamp—to cast a spell that might penetrate the cloud of disenchantment that envelops our world.

The Meanings of Enchantment

When we are enchanted, we are captivated by some part of life—whether it be the fragile charm of the week-old infant or the force of a waterfall that takes our breath away. Enchantment—like the vital energy of Eros—defies definition. We search for synonyms: entrancing, compelling, even haunting. Poetry more often finds the words for this phenomenon. Thus Gerard Manley Hopkins: "The world is charged with the grandeur of God. It will flame out like shining from shook foil."[2] This being *charged*—a painting, a person or the world itself—points, for those with eyes to see, to enchantment. But the very idea of enchantment appears quaint to many in today's world, quarantined in the domain of fairy tales such as *Alice in Wonderland* and *Harry Potter*. Can enchantment point to more than make-believe?

A review of Alice Hoffman's novel, *Nightbird*, suggests the range of this notion. "Alice Hoffman's latest book comes loaded with enchantments. Some are explicitly fantastical: a curse from a brokenhearted witch with real-world consequences, a winged boy who learns the language of birds."[3] There are also more ordinary instances of enchantment. "But some of the magic is of a subtler kind—hours that seem to mysteriously vanish in shared conversation, loneliness transformed by the alchemy of new friendship."[4] In these exchanges neither witches nor goblins are required, but only the *alchemy* of human relationships.

In Hoffman's fictional town, enchantment may be found "not just in the crackle of summer lightning but in ritualistic and common chores—the planting of a garden, the making of a proper pie crust."[5] Enchantment may arise in the most ordinary of actions—a theme that runs through novelist Marilynne Robinson's "rituals of the ordinary."

What enchants? The wonder of nature enchants. "We wonder at what we cannot in any sense incorporate, consume, or encompass in our mental categories; we wonder at mystery, at paradox."[6] We wonder at the immensity of our universe, a reality extravagant and awe inspiring. Wonder grabs our attention, lifting us, however briefly, out of our habitual ways of looking at the world.

Catholic philosopher Charles Taylor links wonder with religious faith. "The wonder [at this world we inhabit] is not only at the stupendous whole, but at the way in which we emerge, in one way fragile and insignificant, and yet capable of grasping this whole."[7] Such an emotion is not far from religious faith: "belonging to the earth, the sense of our dark genesis, can also be part of Christian faith. . . . It is perhaps precisely the ordinary operation of things which constitutes the 'miracle.'"[8]

Beauty, like wonder, serves as threshold to enchantment. Elaine Scarry observes, "It is as though beautiful things have been placed here and there throughout the world to serve as small wake-up calls to perception, spurring lapsed alertness back to its most acute level."[9] She argues that the beauty of the world is such that "if we do not search it out, it comes and finds us."[10] We are entranced by a lovely vase or cuddly pet. Noticing its beauty increases the possibility that we will handle it with care.[11] Beauty, vulnerability and care—the summoning of enchantment.

Religion and Enchantment

Religion, like nature and like art, is dedicated to enchantment. When we become aware of blessings we cannot account for, we are entering an enchanted world. Enchantment in the realm of religion names the epiphanies and graces that find their way into our lives. The Bible teems with enchantment: Moses' burning bush and the manger where Jesus was born are meant to captivate readers.

The Catholic tradition is especially dedicated to enchantment: angels and saints; votive candles and liturgical pageantry; the sacraments as rituals where the sensual opens onto the sacred: all this is enchantment. Andrew Greeley, priest and sociologist, comments, "As Catholics, we find our houses and our world haunted by a sense that the objects, events, and persons of daily life are revelations of grace."[12]

Even in a world become disenchanted, the medieval cathedrals of Europe survive as halls of enchantment. They were designed to charm and lift the human spirit. Their soaring interior spaces and rose windows transfigure our ordinary sense of space and light. Tourists who appreciate these buildings as mere museums are likely to register something of this mysterious appreciation.

As shrines and temples enchant space, religious practices enchant time. The ancient Jews set aside a period called Sabbath; Catholics crafted the Lenten season to reframe time and allow for sober reflection in the midst of busy, distracted lives. At these times and in these places, religious rituals seek to further beguile and charm. Thousands of youths visiting Taizé in France come to the same appreciation. In the incantations of the Taizé liturgy, repeated again and again—"*Ubi caritas, Deus ibi est*" ("Where there is love, there is God") —they enter into moods of becalmed enchantment.

The New Testament captures enchantment in stories of epiphanies and transfigurations. After Jesus died (and there was talk of his appearing to some disciples), his friends went back to earning their livelihoods on the sea. One morning, coming to shore after a night of fishing, they made out a ghostly figure that looked familiar yet unsettling.

> "*Just after daybreak, Jesus stood on the beach; but the disciples did not know that it was Jesus. . . . Jesus said to them, 'Come and have breakfast.' Now none of the disciples dared to ask him, 'Who are you?' because they knew it was the Lord.*" (John 21:4, 12)

Like epiphany, transfiguration names those jolts in consciousness when the ordinary becomes extraordinary.

This occurs when we lift a beautiful cloth from our lap up to the light and its subtly nuanced colors are suddenly revealed. It is the same cloth, yet different now. The stained-glass window does something similar to ordinary light: the illumination on both sides of the window is the same light, yet different. Transfiguration also names the most extraordinary of religious experiences. Two disciples are trudging home to Emmaus, their hearts broken by the death of Jesus. A stranger joins them, questions the cause of their grief, and then takes pains to remind them that this rhythm of death and life has always been the core of their religious heritage. Reaching home, the two disciples invite the stranger to join them for dinner since "it is almost evening and the day is now nearly over." As they share a meal, something astonishing occurs.

> *"When he was at the table with them, he took bread, blessed and broke it and gave it to them. Then their eyes were opened, and they recognized him; and he vanished from their sight."* (Luke 24:30–31)

An epiphany at breakfast and a transfiguration at dinner: memories of meetings that nourish and enchant. A world become enchanted makes possible unexpected blessing: "hours that seem to mysteriously vanish in shared conversation, loneliness transformed by the alchemy of new friendship."[13]

Christianity, as an incarnational faith, celebrates the ordinary with its potential to become extraordinary. It looks to the sensual—water, oil, bread, generous touch—as portal to the sacred, crafting sacraments with just this design. It is convinced that grace springs from every corner of the world, there being no place so distant or so secular that revelation has been excluded. Or, in the words of novelist Marilynne Robinson, "wherever you turn your eyes the world can shine like transfiguration."[14] This is a world lit from within.

Religion in a Disenchanted World

"The goal of the church today must primarily be the re-enchantment of reality." So argues the Catholic author Joseph Bottum, alluding to "the essential God-hauntedness, the enchantment, of the world."[15] When Catholic writers call for "the re-enchantment of reality," they may be alluding to the history of both the Church and western culture in the last five hundred years. Charles Taylor in his masterpiece, *A Secular Age*, has most eloquently detailed the historical evolution of western culture from an enchanted world through a centuries-long period of increasing disenchantment to the yearning today by Christians and others to rediscover the richness and mystery present in a world re-enchanted.

Taylor traces the gradual disenchantment of the western world that was once so thoroughly and vividly enchanted. He recalls life in the year 1500 when every natural event might signal a spiritual message. The comet in the sky or the river's flood was seen as possessing a moral message. Ingmar Bergman celebrated a vision of this enchanted world in his 1960 film *The Virgin Spring*. Set in the fourteenth century, the story recounts the rape and murder of a young woman as she was walking through a forest. After her death, a spring—*a virgin spring*—bubbles up at the death site. In a world enchanted, nature itself weeps for the violence while cleansing the site with this pure water. Natural rhythms utter moral judgments.

This enchanted world began to disappear as two cultural transformations arose to reshape how we saw the world. The great German sociologist Max Weber coined the term "disenchantment" to describe the fruit of the European Enlightenment and the scientific revolution in stripping western Christians of a sense of the world as sacred. When Isaac Newton scientifically demonstrated the colored spectrum of light, earlier religious beliefs about the rainbow as a sacred sign from God lost their persuasiveness. Enchantment was washed out of this colorful celestial display.

The Enlightenment in eighteenth- and nineteenth-century Europe replaced belief in the loving Creator of biblical religions with a more distant Deism. To reason was ceded the realm of science, the natural world, and the public sphere. Religious faith would henceforth exercise its authority in the separate realm of "the supernatural"—a spiritual domain safely distant from the prying eyes of microscope and telescope. Intimidated by the advances of science that often seemed to arise at the expense of religious belief, Christians constructed a firewall between faith and reason. In the words of philosopher of religion Louis Dupré, "[Theologians], afraid that too intimate a connection with material creation would compromise God's absolute transcendence . . . effectively removed God from creation." He adds, "The divine became relegated to a supernatural sphere separate from nature."[16] Grace no longer played throughout creation but was now envisioned as an otherworldly gift to be exported to a darkened natural world. The world was no longer lit from within.

Protestant reformers added their touches to this disenchanted vision of Christian faith. Hoping to cleanse the Catholic tradition of its superstition and corruption, the reformers emptied their churches of ornate sanctuaries, statues of saints, and the smell of incense. These reforms led, in time, to what Charles Taylor has named an *excarnation*—"the transfer of our religious life out of bodily forms of ritual, worship, practice, so that it comes more and more to reside 'in the head.'"[17]

The modern world took shape as a disenchanted place. Gone was the magical harmony of the world and the divine. In such a world—the place where most modern citizens live—*what you see is what you get*. In this disenchanted world, we may appreciate but do not participate: we admire a medieval cathedral as tourists, not believers. We enjoy ancient Christian art, no longer able or willing to be seized by its symbolic resonance with genuine, if hidden, realities.

The disenchantment growing over the last several centuries has taken an enormous toll on religion. Atheists from Friedrich Nietzsche to Christopher Hitchens proclaimed the death of God; Marxism forecast the end of religion. For many people this desert of criticism endures, with its sense that the world is what we see and nothing more. Despite this pervasive mood of disenchantment in modern life, many Christians cling to a conviction, however tentative and unclear, that there is here *more than meets the eye*. And beyond the believing community, many today are recovering a sense of the mystery in the world. The planet we inhabit—that charming "blue marble" displayed to us by circling astronauts—now seems to be more than mute matter running according to the rigid rules of physics. Its fragility and vulnerability—suspended out there with no visible means of support—are newly appreciated.

Catholic worship is likewise returning to a sense of enchantment in its liturgical life. In the years since the Second Vatican Council, Catholics have come to appreciate how the mysterious workings of grace move through the ordinary elements of water, oil, and bread as they are transfigured into sacraments of welcome in Baptism, of healing in the Anointing of the Sick, and of nourishment in the Eucharist. Sacraments are exercises in sacred enchantment: the ordinary is transfigured into the extraordinary.

Paradoxically, it is the very advance of science that is opening the door, once again, to enchantment. Rachel Carson's 1962 analysis of pesticides in *Silent Spring* invited readers to see the land we plow and plant not as inert dirt but as living soil. Once we see the soil as a vibrant environment teeming with life, our eyes are opened to its charming fragility and we begin to exercise a new level of care. Carson's *silent spring* echoes Bergman's *virgin spring*: a once-vital water source gone silent from human poisoning.

A God-Haunted World

Catholics are finding comfort in metaphors of God's presence in creation that had once been outlawed. Dorothy Day wrote, "'All my life I have been haunted by

God.'"[18] Theater critic John Lahr, observing the role of ghosts in dramas, asks, "Can we agree that we're all haunted? The ghost world is part of our world. We carry within us the good and the bad, the spoken and the unspoken imperatives of our missing loved ones." He adds, "Conversations rarely stop at the grave. So when we encounter ghosts onstage, they both terrify and compel us; within their trapped energy is an echo of our own unresolved losses."[19]

Modern sensibilities—with biases toward rationality and scientific analysis—recoil at the image of "haunting." The advances of the Enlightenment and the social progress it initiated seemed to have permanently banished the ghosts that had inhabited and inhibited so much of premodern life. And yet the ghosts will not disappear.

The world of art has always been more comfortable with the notion of haunting realities. Viewing an impressive painting, we are made aware of a mood or suggestion that somehow *inhabits* this picture. We cannot directly describe for ourselves, nor convincingly point out to someone else, this intimation of meaning. Yet some compelling information has made its way, unbidden, into our consciousness. The artist has so arranged the light and shadow as to elicit a mood or emotion that we may say now "haunts" the picture.

It is this quality of experience that art critic Peter Schjeldahl seeks to evoke in his description of the art of the Spanish painter El Greco: "The glory and the problem of El Greco is the same: spirituality . . . the awareness that glimmers at the head-spring of consciousness, prior to thought and feeling—as the primary fact of life, always on tap."[20] Schjeldahl concludes, "Spiritual intimations trickle through all minds, however obscurely, and even while discounted or ignored."[21] So it is with beautiful music: beyond the tones that can be scientifically described, we become attentive to something more and something else—easy to experience yet difficult to name. Literary critic George Steiner describes such *annunciations*: "That which comes to call on us . . . will very often do so unbidden. Even when there is a readiness, as in the concert hall, in the museum, in the moment of chosen reading, the true entrance into us will not occur by an act of will."[22]

Marking the metaphors that Catholic novelists choose in describing the enchantment of their faith will illumine the arc of the Catholic imagination through the course of the twentieth century. From the darker images of Evelyn Waugh (human enchantments that cannot endure) and Graham Greene (bargains with God we cannot keep), we come to the more optimistic metaphors of Thomas Merton and Dorothy Day (both failed novelists) as they encourage Catholics toward an engagement with society in pursuit of a more just world. In later decades, novelists Mary Gordon and Marilynne Robinson (a card-carrying Calvinist to whom we are granting honorary status as Catholic) deploy metaphors of water, light, and even laughter that celebrate the sacramental conviction of the sensual as portal to the sacred. The arc of the Catholic imagination across the century moves from a vision of grace as imported to a world disenchanted and darkened by sin toward a more optimistic view of a world lit from within.

[1] Evelyn Waugh, *Brideshead Revisited*, 31.
[2] Gerard Manley Hopkins, "God's Grandeur," *The Major Works*, 114.
[3] Leigh Bardugo, "Alice Hoffman's 'Nightbird,'" *The New York Times Sunday Book Review*.
[4] Bardugo.
[5] Bardugo.
[6] Caroline Walker Bynum, *Metamorphosis and Identity*, 53.
[7] Charles Taylor, *A Secular Age*, 606.
[8] Taylor, *A Secular Age*, 548.
[9] Elaine Scarry, *On Beauty and Being Just*, 81.
[10] Scarry.
[11] Scarry, 80.
[12] Andrew Greeley, *The Catholic Imagination*, 1. Greeley's remark about Catholics at the beginning of this chapter is from p. 184.
[13] Bardugo.
[14] Marilynne Robinson, *Gilead*, 245.
[15] Joseph Bottum, "The Things We Share," *Commonweal*.
[16] Louis Dupré, *Passage to Modernity*, 3.
[17] Taylor, *A Secular Age*, 613.
[18] Dorothy Day, *The Long Loneliness*, 11.
[19] John Lahr, "Trapped in Time: 'Mary Rose' and "Salvage,'" *The New Yorker*, 92.
[20] Peter Schjeldahl, "El Greco at the Met," *The New Yorker*, 198.
[21] Schjeldahl.
[22] George Steiner, *Real Presences*, 179.

Part One

❦

Catholic Faith within a Disenchanted World

In 1922, T. S. Eliot and James Joyce raised the bar for literary enchantment. Eliot's *The Waste Land* evoked the disenchantment of his post-World War I era. Joyce's *Ulysses* conjured the enchantment of the city he both loved and loathed. Eight years later, Eliot would write *Ash Wednesday* to express his newfound enchantment with his Anglican faith.

Both authors, the Anglo-Catholic Eliot and the renegade Catholic Joyce, helped themselves to the language and symbolism of Catholic faith to charm their audiences with radically novel portraits of life in a disenchanted world.

That same year, Evelyn Waugh and Graham Greene were students at Oxford, hatching their own literary careers. Several years later each would enter the Catholic Church, and by mid-century each would be producing novels—especially *Brideshead Revisited* and *The End of the Affair*—that were steeped in Catholic imagery.

In these same decades, two French Catholic novelists—Georges Bernanos and François Mauriac—were composing fiction that explored how their faith could survives in a world grown disenchanted. Mauriac's definition of the novel describes the efforts of all these writers: "To light up the secret sources of sanctity in creatures which seem to us to have failed."[1]

[1] Ralph McInerny, *Some Catholic Writers*, 92.

Chapter One
Ashes to Ashes, Dust to Dust

"I will show you fear in a handful of dust."

—T. S. Eliot

In *The Waste Land*, T. S. Eliot spelled out the cultural desolation that had settled over England and Europe after the horrors of a world war. With the many millions of deaths, the war had ground down the optimism of western culture into "a handful of dust."[1] In the disillusionment that settled over postwar Europe, there seemed to be little room for religious belief or for prayer of any kind. Dust was the residue of vanquished hopes; ash was the deathly detritus of a world grown disenchanted.

Six years after the publication of *The Waste Land*, Eliot would enter the Anglican Church, embracing the liturgical rituals of Anglo-Catholics. Captivated by the ceremonies in this religious heritage, he would write *Ash Wednesday*, a poem and prayer that celebrates his returning belief in enchantment. In this poem, the "dust" of *The Waste Land* is transfigured into the enchanted "ashes" of a Lenten ritual.

The Christian celebration of Ash Wednesday that opens the season of Lent centers on the ritual application of a thumb smudge of ashes on a person's forehead, accompanied by the prayer, "Remember, O human, that you are dust and unto dust you will return." (In his day the prayer was spoken in Latin: *memento homo, quia pulvis es et in pulverem reverteris*). The ritual echoes the passage in the book of Genesis where God banishes the first couple from Eden with the reminder, "By the sweat of your face you shall eat bread until you return to the ground, for out of it you were taken; you are dust and to dust you shall return." (Genesis 3:19)

In his poem, Eliot has reimagined the "dust" of *The Waste Land* not as symbol of utter ruination but as "ashes" that serve as reminder of our earthly origins and our mortality. Ashes, stark symbol of destruction—the fire burned down, all heat and vitality extinguished— are transfigured until they ignite, paradoxically, aspirations for life beyond these cinders.

In *Small Victories*, essayist Anne Lamott meditates on this liturgical ceremony. "Ash Wednesday came early this year. It was supposed to be about preparation, about consecration, about moving toward Easter, toward resurrection and renewal."[2] She attempts to explain the day to her young son. "We daub our foreheads with ashes, I explained, because they remind us of how much we miss and celebrate those who have already died. The ashes remind us of the finality of death . . . and so people also mark themselves with ashes to show that they trust in the alchemy God can work with those ashes—jogging us awake, moving us toward greater attention and openness and love."[3]

Christian authors seem particularly attracted to ashes. Marilynne Robinson, in her novel *Gilead*, creates a portrait of a group of Christians coming together in response to a church that has burned to the ground. Ashes are everywhere and, in the midst of the cleanup, a father gives his son a biscuit tinged with this ash.

Years later, the son remembers this nourishment from his father's dirty hands as a kind of communion, the ashes—enchanted now—only adding to what Robinson calls "a ritual of the ordinary."[4]

In the final rapturous paragraphs of his *Divine Milieu*, Pierre Teilhard de Chardin brings dust and enchantment together. "Now the earth can certainly grasp me in her giant arms. She can swell me with her life, or take me back into her dust. . . . But her enchantments can no longer do me harm, since she has become for me, over and above herself, the body of him who is and him who is coming. The *divine milieu*."[5]

In the alchemy of both literature and religious ritual, ashes are transfigured into something more than mere burnt-out matter. They are made sober reminders of undying hopes that mark our mortality; they become enchanted.

Darkness That Enchants

In a few lines of "East Coker" in *Four Quartets*, Eliot provides a master class in the poetic techniques of enchantment. He captures the moment when an audience sits quietly in the dark between acts of a theatrical drama. This is a darkness that neither blinds nor threatens; rather, all is anticipation: sitting among others in the dark, we wait for the curtain to once again rise.

In this moment of stillness, the audience may hear backstage bustle as scenery is moved. "As, in a theatre / The lights are extinguished, for the scene to be changed / With a hollow rumble of wings, with a movement of darkness on darkness. . . ."[6] Artistic and religious sensibilities merge in the theater of Eliot's imagination. The "hollow rumble of wings" is most likely stagehands behind the curtain arranging the new set. Or, for more excited imaginations, it may be the flutter of wings of angels, patrons of the production.

There is darkness that signals the end of seeing, the extermination of light. And there is darkness whose business is anticipation. "I said to my soul, be still, and let the dark come upon you / Which shall be the darkness of God."[7] Eliot alludes to "the darkness of God"—the night of the soul that John of the Cross so brightly illuminated. Here, too, darkness frames the interval when the next stage of life, not yet visible, is being crafted. Darkness, negative symbol of light lost, is here transformed. Like ashes, darkness now glows with enchantment.

Redeeming the Time

The art of poetry is the transformation of the ordinary—ashes, darkness—into something else and something more. The charm of symbols is that they do not banish the ordinary, but open it to something more. Symbols manage to mean more than they say. So it is with the ordinary yet mysterious unfolding of time. Eliot's poetry circles again and again around this puzzle. He is in search of the "still point of the turning world"[8] where time pivots from past to future.

In *The Waste Land*, Eliot has meditated on the fraught period after World War I and the poem began with a reference to time: "April is the cruelest month." In *Ash Wednesday*, Eliot framed the search for a religious re-enchantment in the scriptural phrase, "redeem the time." (Eph 5:16, King James Version) From what is time to be redeemed? From time made murderous in war? Time wasted or simply allowed to drain away?

In *The Four Quartets*, Eliot increases his devotion to time redeemed. The first poem, *Burnt Norton*, declares, "If all time is eternally present / All time is irredeemable."[9] The challenge is not to escape time (there is no place to go) nor to defeat it, but to inhabit it with wit and presence of mind.

If time in the twentieth century is disenchanted like every other part of life, the challenge is to again make something meaningful, something holy of it; to discover its potential enchantment. Ash Wednesday—the liturgical celebration—breaks into the ordinary flow of days, initiating a time of new alertness in preparation for Easter. The Lenten season measures time, lifting it out of a chronic more-of-the-same. And the liturgical year of Christian faith in which Ash Wednesday and Lent are embedded offers a distinctive alternative to the endless recycling of seasons in an effort to "redeem the time."

Ashes, darkness, and time may be recruited to frame religious belief. To the disenchanted, ash is merely inert detritus, devoid of promise; darkness is deficit and lack of illumination; time merely marks the chronic unwinding of our lives and our return to dust and darkness. In literature and religious ritual, creative artists strive to invest ashes and darkness and time with more meaning than they might seem to possess. Transfiguring these elements of ordinary life, literature and religion enchant our world.

James Joyce: "An Enchantment of the Heart"

In the midst of Joyce's autobiographical novel, *Portrait of the Artist as a Young Man,* Stephen Daedalus awakes from a delicious dream about the girl he was eyeing at university the day before. The sleeping fantasy from which he has only half awoken strikes him as "an enchantment of the heart": "He lay still, as if his soul lay among cool waters, conscious of faint, sweet music."[10]

In this episode, the themes of enchantment and the Catholic imagination come together. Joyce resorts, as usual, to images and metaphors from the faith he has so insistently rejected. Angels—"seraphim"—are invoked repeatedly. The spontaneity of the dream seems virginal: "In the virgin womb of the imagination the word was made flesh."[11] He seems to hear a poem that warns of "ardent ways" and counsels, "Tell no more of enchanted days."[12] His overheated imagination then pictures "incense ascending from the altar of the world."[13] The earth itself, in the middle of this fantasy, "was like a swinging smoking swaying censer, a ball of incense."[14] Catholic readers would have been most familiar with this image of the priest at the altar swinging the censer from which billows of incense smoke arose. Joyce, rejecting his Catholic faith, cannot do without its language. Joyce even has a companion of Stephen point this out: "It is a curious thing, do you know, Cranly said dispassionately, how your mind is supersaturated with the religion in which you say you disbelieve."[15]

This novel is a coming-of-age story of a youth who is laboring to extract himself from the mire of his Irish heritage and Catholic piety to become a self-made creative artist. Joyce rearranges the scraps of his Catholic youth to conjure a "portrait" of the person he hopes to become. Its hero, Stephen Daedalus (the name unites the early Christian martyr, St. Stephen, and Daedalus of Greek myth), struggles to cast off the smothering culture and faith of his youth.

The agenda of the novel is all enchantment as Stephen strives to charm his artist-self into existence. "He wanted to meet in the real world the unsubstantial image which his soul so constantly beheld."[16] If Stephen could but meet this hoped-for self, he and his ideal "would be alone, surrounded by darkness and silence: and in that moment of supreme tenderness he would be transfigured."[17] Finally becoming the "artist" he always knew he would become, "weakness and timidity and inexperience would fall from him in that magic moment."[18] Joyce's language of "transfigure" and "magic" is the currency of enchantment.

Stephen muses on his race and its religiousness: "the broken lights of Irish myth" [broken by English rule] and "the Roman catholic religion" have both led to "the attitude of a dull-witted loyal serf."[19] He regrets the historical abuse his nation has suffered. "When the soul of a man is born in this country there are nets flung at it to hold it back from flight. You talk to me of nationality, language, religion. I shall try to fly by those nets."[20] The "net" of his disavowed Catholic faith is a web to be escaped, but also a net filled to overflowing with literary resources—all the imagery and metaphors of this religion that he will tirelessly deploy to craft his stories.

As the novel ends, Stephen has determined that he must, like every heroic artist, go into exile. "Probably I shall go away," says Stephen.[21] He "will not serve" church or nation, but journey on alone, with only his "silence, exile, and cunning."[22] Biographer Richard Ellmann interprets this self-exiling. "Joyce needed exile as a reproach to others and a justification of himself . . . like other revolutionaries, he fattened on opposition and grew thin and pale when treated with indulgence."[23] For Joyce, "writing itself was a form of exile for him, a source of detachment."[24] Literary critic Anthony Burgess argues that Joyce ended his days, after all this talk of exile, as "a walking-guide to Dublin past and present, an expatriate Irishman, a Mass-missing Catholic who knew as much as the priests."[25]

A Haunted World

"The Dead," the last story in Joyce's *Dubliners,* turns to a theme important to many of the Catholic writers in the twentieth century. After a party celebrating the feast of the Epiphany, a young husband, Gabriel, and his wife, Gretta, prepare to retire for the night. She is suddenly overcome, remembering a song that another young man had sung to her during a brief, teenage romance. When she tells her husband of this memory, Gabriel is moved with anger. That young man, who had died at age seventeen, lived on in his wife's memory, generating feelings of jealousy in Gabriel. How was Gabriel to compete with such a ghostly existence?

Gretta, spent by the sad memories of that teenage romance, falls asleep. Gabriel is left to sort out the multiple painful emotions surging through him. For his own consolation, he muses on the reality that each of them, in their own time, will die. "One by one, they were all becoming shades." His confusing emotions give way to "generous tears."[26] Joyce writes, "His soul had approached that region where dwell the vast hosts of the dead."[27] Anthony Burgess comments, "That world goes on with its own life, and its purpose is . . . to haunt the world of those not yet gone."[28] The story ends as Gabriel lets go of the usual distinction between living and deceased. He falls asleep with "the snow falling faintly through the universe and faintly falling, like the descent of their last end, upon all the living and the dead."[29]

Richard Ellmann situates this haunting in Joyce's writing: "That the dead do not stay buried is, in fact, a theme of Joyce from the beginning to the end of his work."[30] Joyce's "head was filled with a sense of the too successful encroachment of the dead upon the living city; there was a disruptive parallel in the way that Dublin, buried behind him, was haunting his thoughts."[31]

Modern science and reason leave little room for haunting. A disenchanted world has no category for such reveries. Yet the world of literature, as well as that of religion, cannot do without appeal to all that haunts this world. How to express the continuing presence of what is assumed to be absent? Of persons and plans that are gone but not extinct? Of the afterlife of hopes and ideals that we thought we had bid adieu?

Joyce's *Ulysses*: Enchanting Dublin

In *Ulysses*, Joyce will employ his Catholic imagination to create out of his hometown the enchanted city of Dublin. In the opening scene, one of Stephen Daedalus' college dormmates, Buck Mulligan, enters their common room while reciting with mock solemnity, *introibo ad altare Dei* ("I will go onto the altar of God")—the prayer that began the Catholic Mass, still celebrated in Latin at that time. Mulligan is wearing his "yellow dressing gown," like the long alb that the priest at Mass would wear. Then he "blessed gravely thrice the tower, the surrounding land and the awakening mountains."[32] The novel begins the way the Catholic Mass begins. Anthony Burgess suggests Joyce's meaning here: "A rite of solemn meaning . . . is about to begin."[33] The scene is one of student-style mockery, but as so often in Joyce, is about more than levity.

In this novel, Joyce is creating a fever-dream of events taking place within a single day in his hometown that he both loves and detests. His intent is to raise up Dublin in all its mortality—light and dark, urine and snot—to a kind of literary immortality. Literary critic Louis Menand, observing that "*Ulysses* begins with a mock celebration of the Eucharist," argues that we see here "that literary representation is an act of transubstantiation. Literature pulls the real up out of the realm of temporality and insignificance and remakes it into a form that will never decay and never die."[34] We are witnesses here to the literary machinery of enchantment.

Anthony Burgess, himself a British Catholic novelist, goes Menand one better. In his reading, Joyce enchants by "solemnizing" dates and places of everyday life. Think of the Dublin of *Ulysses* and the yearly commemoration of Bloomsday (June 16, 1904, the day the novel took place). "Joyce, without blasphemy, saw his function as priestlike—the solemnization of drab days and the sanctification of the ordinary."[35] Burgess presses his point about Joyce relishing the richness of the ordinary: "Ordinary people, living in an ordinary city, are invested in the richness of the ages, and these riches are enshrined in language, which is available to everybody."[36] Burgess then reframes his judgment in more religious language: "the discovery of epiphanies—'showings forth'—of beauty and truth in the squalid and commonplace was Joyce's vocation."[37] Epiphany is, of course, the religious language of enchantment.

For Burgess, Joyce's art is that of a priest: at the conclusion of *Portrait* "Stephen at last knows that literature is his vocation, priestly enough since its function is the transmutation of lowly accidents to godly essence."[38] Both artists and priests are the chief conjurers and chief enchanters for society.

Fervent (Renegade) Catholic

Devoted to his teachers while loathing the spiritual heritage they represented, Joyce could see himself as a Jesuit without being a Catholic. In such self-imagining, Joyce defined his love/hate relationship with his Irish Catholic heritage. Throughout his life, Joyce kept leaving Ireland and then returning to it—most dramatically in his novel, *Ulysses*. Joyce kept eschewing his religious faith, then returning to it to ransack its rich imagery.

In self-imposed exile from his homeland, he writes only of Ireland, transforming his rejected Dublin into an enchanted city. Abandoning his Catholicism, the faith of his childhood and nation, he constantly draws on its symbols as a kind of second language. Anthony Burgess: "Joyce's attitude toward Catholicism is the familiar love-hate one of most renegades. He has left the Church, but he cannot leave it alone."[39]

Biographer Richard Ellmann judges: "Christianity has subtly evolved in his mind from a religion into a system of metaphors, which as metaphors could claim his fierce allegiance."[40] He adds, "He was no longer a Christian himself; but he converted the temple to new uses instead of trying to knock it down, regarding it as a superior kind of folly and one which, interpreted by a secular artist, contained obscure bits of truth."[41]

Both Eliot and Joyce cast themselves as outsiders and exiles. The America-born Eliot defined himself as "resident alien" in England. Joyce rejoiced in his exile status that gave him the distance to see more clearly the place and faith he would reject and then enchant. This "outsider" status will become a regular characteristic of Catholic writers in the first half of the century.

Afterthoughts

Thomas Sterns Eliot (1888–1965) began life in St. Louis, Missouri, in a family that belonged to the Unitarian church. At Harvard, he discovered the world of the literary elite, and in England he found among Anglicans the spiritual belonging that fit his temperament. He described himself as having a "Catholic cast of mind, a Calvinist heritage, and a Puritanical temperament."[42]

Eliot was both an elitist and a bit of a poseur. "Eliot was then a master of disguise or protective camouflage—an upper-class Englishman with his publishing colleagues, a Yankee with Yankees and indeed a pillar of the Church with other such pillars."[43]

He received the Nobel Prize for Literature in 1948, and as an international celebrity, he was called upon to lecture on Christianity and culture. Peter Ackroyd remarks, "in his social criticism Eliot assumes an idea of England which never existed and proposes an England which could not exist."[44]

After a long and miserable marriage, he married a second time in 1957 when he was sixty-eight, and his new wife, his secretary at the publishing house of Faber and Faber, was thirty. He died in 1965, a year before Evelyn Waugh.

James Joyce was born on February 2, 1882, the feast of Candlemas, and Groundhog Day. He was the oldest of ten surviving children, two died of typhoid. After his early schooling with the Jesuits (beginning his long-running romance with this Order), he entered University College Dublin. His initial vocational interest was medicine. Richard Ellmann observes, "The writer, who had Ireland for patient, to anatomize and purge, might plausibly be physician too. Such a conjunction helped lure Joyce on to what did not prove 'a brilliant career' in medicine."[45]

In January 1904, Joyce dashed off an essay on the artist as a young man. He would redraft this auto-biographic essay in *Stephen Hero* and again as *A Portrait of the Artist as a Young Man*. That same year, he met his future wife, Nora Barnacle. They would soon leave for Europe (the lifelong exile begins). Finding a job teaching English for Berlitz in Trieste, he spent most of his twenties in that Italian city. In 1915, with the war on, Joyce and family moved to Zurich. He struggled to get *A Portrait* published in book form, meeting great resistance. Meanwhile, his collection of short stories, *Dubliners*, found very few buyers in its first years. In 1939, he published *Finnegans Wake*; and in 1941, Joyce died of peritonitis (a perforated ulcer) at age fifty-eight.

1   T. S. Eliot, *The Waste Land*, 54.
2   Anne Lamott, *Small Victories*, 119.
3   Lamott.
4   Marilynne Robinson, *Gilead*, 95.
5   Teilhard de Chardin, *The Divine Milieu*, 134.
6   Eliot, "East Coker," *Four Quartets*, 186.
7   Eliot, Four Quartets.
8   T. S. Eliot, "Burnt Norton," *Four Quartets*, 177.
9   Eliot, *Four Quartets*, 175.
10 James Joyce, *A Portrait of the Artist as a Young Man*, 235.
11 Joyce, *Portrait*, 236.
12 Joyce, *Portrait*.
13 Joyce, *Portrait*.
14 Joyce, *Portrait*.
15 Joyce, *Portrait*, 261.
16 Joyce, *Portrait*, 67.
17 Joyce, *Portrait*.
18 Joyce, *Portrait*.
19 Joyce, *Portrait*, 195.
20 Joyce, *Portrait*, 220.
21 Joyce, *Portrait*, 267.
22 Joyce, *Portrait*, 269.
23 Richard Ellmann, *James Joyce*, 109.
24 Ellmann, 110.
25 Anthony Burgess, *Here Comes Everybody*, 27.
26 James Joyce, "The Dead," in *Dubliners*, 191
27 Joyce, 191–2.
28 Burgess, 44
29 Joyce, 192.
30 Ellmann, 244.
31 Ellmann.
32 James Joyce, *Ulysses*, 3.
33 Burgess, 32.
34 Louis Menand, "Adam Begley's 'Updike,'" *The New Yorker*, 76.
35 Burgess, 25
36 Burgess.
37 Burgess, 17.
38 Burgess, 56.
39 Burgess, 32.
40 Richard Ellmann, 66.
41 Ellmann.
42 T. S. Eliot, *On Poetry and Poets*, 209.
43 Peter Ackroyd, *T. S. Eliot*, 236.
44 Ackroyd, 313.
45 Ellmann, 97.

Chapter Two
Enchantments Faux and Genuine

Evelyn Waugh's 1945 masterpiece, *Brideshead Revisited*, is a religion-obsessed and God-haunted novel. The novel is also a fable about enchantments, human and divine. Part One describes the enchantment that Charles Ryder experiences as he falls in with the charming Sebastian Flyte, son of a rich, eccentric Catholic family. This is an adolescent romance built on skipped classes and picnics of strawberries and champagne. And it is an enchantment resting on Sebastian's fragile beauty. "He was magically beautiful, with that epicene quality which in extreme youth sings loud for love and withers at the first cold wind."[1] By the end of Part One, such a "first cold wind" had arisen and this enchantment had begun to wither.

In Part Two, Charles Ryder enters into an adulterous affair with Sebastian's sister, Julia. But Julia's Catholic faith means this enchantment cannot endure. Waugh enlists nature to announce its imminent end: Charles and Julia walk through the gardens at Brideshead in the late afternoon: it was "already in twilight, but the lakes below us were aflame; the light grew in strength and splendour as it neared death."[2]

As the novel concludes, Charles, now a world-weary soldier, returns to Brideshead and finds, to his surprise, that the sanctuary lamp in the Marchmain's once-shuttered chapel has been lit again. The lamp, extinguished countless times in history and relit once again, represents to Charles—and to Waugh—a sacred enchantment that outlasts every human frailty.

Enchantments within a Disenchanted World

The prologue opens on a scene of disenchantment. Captain Charles Ryder has been stationed for three months with his troops in a rural setting in England. Waiting resignedly for orders, he muses on his falling out of love with the military. And he realizes that something has died within him and, at the age of thirty-nine, he has become old.

In the midst of this mood of disillusionment, Charles hears his commanding officer mention the nearby Brideshead estate. He is startled, and memories of his halcyon days with Sebastian rush forth. "He had spoken a name that was so familiar to me, a conjurer's name of such ancient power, that, at its mere sound, the phantoms of those haunted late years began to take flight."[3] Waugh's choice of imagery—"a conjurer's name" and "those haunted years"—ushers us into this tale of multiple enchantments.

Waugh signals the shadows that must haunt every human enchantment with the title of Part One: *Et in Arcadia Ego*. This Latin phrase (in English, "I too was

there in that Edenic place") was associated with a painting by the sixteenth-century artist Nicolas Poussin that
showed idealized youths standing in a pastoral setting
next to a tomb. The painting was seen as a *memento
mori*, with the speaker being death. The message: in
every enchanted garden lurk reminders of our mortality. Human enchantments, whatever their temporary
charm, cannot endure. Waugh then tells the story of
two romances that must necessarily fail. He will follow
these cautionary tales with two instances of the genuine, sacred enchantment that he believes lies at the
heart of the Catholic faith.

The story proper begins as Charles's memory fills
with the emotions that marked those early days as a fellow student with Sebastian. Waugh captures the mood
with his description of a perfect day in Oxford: "It was
a day of peculiar splendor, such as our climate allows
once or twice a year, when leaf and flower and bird and
sun-lit stone and shadow all seem to proclaim the glory
of God."[4] The enchantment that will possess Sebastian
Flyte and Charles Ryder in their brief days together will
take place in the city of Oxford in the year 1922: "a city of
aquatint" where people walked and spoke as they did in
Cardinal Newman's time; a place that "exhaled the soft
vapours of a thousand years of learning."[5] In this idyllic
scene, Charles meets Sebastian for the first time, but
even before this encounter, Sebastian was well known
to many at Oxford. "He was the most conspicuous man
of his year by reason of his beauty, which was arrest-
ing, and his eccentricities of behavior which seemed to
know no bounds."[6] Sebastian—Lord Sebastian Flyte,
the second son of the Marquis of Marchmain—meeting

Charles, insists, "You're to come away at once, out of danger. (A swarm of women are visiting the university buildings.) I've got a motor-car and a basket of straw-berries and a bottle of Chateau Peyraguey—which isn't a wine you've ever tasted, so don't pretend. It's heaven with strawberries."[7]

Charles is swept away by the charming Sebastian. "I was in search of love in those days, and I went full of curiosity" and the hope that "I should find that low door in the wall . . . which opened on an enclosed and enchanted garden."[8]

The two spend the summer vacation "alone together" at Brideshead in the absence of Sebastian's family. But this time-out-of-time cannot endure, and as the summer ends, they return to Oxford. Years later, looking back at the earlier idyllic time, Charles reflects, "It is thus I like to remember Sebastian, as he was that summer, when we wandered alone together through that enchanted palace."[9]

Their return to Oxford in October signals a shift, again marked by the weather: "the autumnal mood possessed us both as though the riotous exuberance of June had died."[10] Sebastian senses some larger ending: "I feel so old . . . I believe we have had all the fun we can expect here."[11] During this fall term, the two of them "lived more and more in the shadows."[12]

Their other classmates were now settling down and taking their studies seriously. "They lumbered back into the herd from which they had been so capriciously cho-sen and grew less and less individually recognizable."[13] The affection that Charles and Sebastian had shared so intensely began to wane. Back at Oxford, "we took up again the life that seemed to be shrinking in the cold air."[14] Sebastian "was sick at heart somewhere, I did not know how and I grieved for him, unable to help."[15] Now Sebastian was drinking excessively, not out of high spirits, but to escape the fate that his very religious but dysfunctional family seemed to prescribe.

Lady Marchmain invites Charles to join the family at Brideshead for the Christmas vacation, hoping that he can influence Sebastian, who has fallen ever deeper into alcoholism. But as Charles is drawn into the family, Sebastian grows more distant. When Charles, against his own best judgment, gives money to Sebastian to buy more alcohol, Lady Marchmain expresses her deep regret at this "betrayal" of her. Charles departs from Brideshead, seemingly for the last time. "I felt that I was leaving part of myself behind, and that wherever I went afterwards I should feel the lack of it." Waugh again summons the image of enchantment: "A door had shut, the low door in the wall I had sought and found in Oxford: open it now and I should find no enchanted garden." Charles tells himself, "I have left behind illusion. . . . Henceforth I live in a world of three dimensions—with the aid of my five senses." Resigned to a world of disenchantment he would later come to understand, "I have since learned that there is no such world."[16]

Another Enchantment: The Affair of Charles and Julia

As Part Two opens, the reader meets Charles in his new vocation as architectural painter. He has become wealthy painting classic buildings in England just as

they were about to be destroyed and replaced with sub-
urban developments and shopping centers—"to salute
their achievements at the moment of their extinc-
tion."[17] His very success was, ironically, "a symptom of
the decline."[18] Reflecting on his success in this disenchanted world, Charles grieves again the loss of that
romantic period in his youth. "But as the years passed
I began to mourn the loss of something I had known
in the drawing-room of Marchmain House and once or
twice since, the intensity and singleness and the belief
that it was not all done by hand—in a word, the inspiration."[19] Inspiration here stands as synonym for the
enchantment that had been all but drained from his life.

As Part Two unfolds, we learn that both Charles and
Julia, now in the midst of an affair, are still married to
other partners. Charles's wife, Celia, had borne two children even as their marriage had begun to disintegrate.
Meanwhile, Julia had married Rex Mottram, a blunt,
loud, and rich Canadian—"a colonial."[20] Their marriage
had likewise come to naught. Both Charles and Julia are
now returning—coincidentally on the same ship—to
England from America after Charles had finished several years painting in South America and after Julia had
ended a sexual fling. Thrown together onboard, they
begin their affair and Charles observed how the once
nineteen-year-old Julia's beauty had matured. She had
added a "haunting, magical sadness which spoke straight
to the heart and struck silence; it was the completion of
her beauty."[21] In Waugh's Catholic imagination, beauty
and sadness are conjoined in every human enchantment.

The reader next meets Julia as this nineteen-year-old
beauty who is trying to decide if there were any likely

Catholic candidates for her to marry. "But wherever she turned, it seemed, her religion stood as a barrier between her and her natural goal."[22] While dating Rex, she asks a Jesuit confessor if it wouldn't be so wrong to live with him before marriage. The priest tells Julia it would be wrong and "from that moment she shut her mind against her religion."[23]

Returning to their liaison, Waugh observes this enchantment continuing beyond the ocean crossing. When their tryst returns to Brideshead, Julia tells Charles, "I feel as though all mankind and God, too, were in a conspiracy against us." She asks, "They can't hurt us, can they? Not tonight; not now."[24] This "us against the world" attitude of the two lovers repeats the vow that Sebastian and Charles had sworn of their own conspiracy *"contra mundum."* As their time together in this lovely setting comes to an end, the day was "already in twilight, but the lakes below us were aflame; the light grew in strength and splendour as it neared death."[25] Nature itself laments the enchantment of their liaison as it approaches its end.

Beset by guilt, Julia moves to break off the affair. For her to continue in this sinful liaison with Charles would be "to set up a rival good to God's."[26] She names her decision "a private bargain between me and God; that if I give up this one thing I want so much, however bad I am, He won't quite despair of me in the end."[27]

Two Sacred Enchantments

Julia's crisis of faith signals another set of enchantments available to her as a Catholic, even a sinful one. Waugh signals the appearance of these sacred enchantments with the title of the Part Two of the novel: "A Twitch Upon the Thread." Sebastian's younger sister, Cordelia, informs Charles about her mother's habit of reading to the family from G. K. Chesterton's stories of Father Brown. In one of these stories, the fictional priest-detective captures a criminal he had been tracking. "I caught him [the thief] with an unseen hook and an invisible line which is long enough to let him wander to the ends of the world and still to bring him back with *a twitch upon the thread.*"[28] Waugh turns this image to his own purposes as a description of God who allows sinners to do their worst before finally rescuing them from their sinful ways with "a twitch upon the thread." Cordelia comments on her family's waywardness: "God won't let them go for long, you know,"[29] but will pull them with this thread back from their sinfulness.

One sacred enchantment that the Catholic faith made available to sinners was "the last sacraments." (Catholic authors Waugh and Graham Greene knew this sacrament as Extreme Unction: a priest-administered anointing (thus, *Unction*) that followed Confession and reception of the Blessed Sacrament at the point of death (thus, *Extreme*). Sebastian's mother received the last sacraments just before her death. When Sebastian's father returns from his adulterous life in Venice to die at Brideshead, the family gathers around, waiting and hoping that the dying man will give some sign of repentance for his sinful life. A priest arrives and is sent away. Now even the agnostic Charles offers a prayer: "Then I knelt, too, and prayed, 'O God, if there is a God, forgive him his sins, if there is such a thing as sin.'"[30] Again the priest comes, and finally the old man gives a sign of his repentance and the priest is able to anoint him. He breathes his last, and the family gives thanks that the old man has narrowly escaped eternal punishment.

Waugh is describing what might be called the spirituality of ultimate anxiety that enjoyed prominence in the first half of twentieth-century Catholicism. God was pictured as "the hound of heaven" and stern judge who will separate the sheep from the goats at the end of time (Matthew 25). Catholic preachers during these decades emphasized "the four last things"—death, judgment, heaven, and hell. Catholics learned to be anxious about their deaths that might catch them in sin and so render them worthy of eternal damnation. Julia admits to this anxiety: "I can't get all that sort of thing out of my mind, quite—death, judgment, Heaven, Hell, Nanny Hawkins and the Catechism."[31] The funeral liturgy in the first half of the century reinforced this anxiety about death and judgment: the casket was draped in black and the celebrant wore black vestments. The hymn that dominated the service was *Dies Irae, Dies Illa* (*Day of Wrath, Fateful Day*).

The transformative importance of this sacrament of forgiveness and blessing comes to prominence in Cordelia's account of the likely scenario of Sebastian's sordid and alcoholic death. "Then one morning, after one of his drinking bouts, he'll be picked up at the gate dying, and show by a mere flicker of the eyelid that he is conscious when they give him the last sacraments." Then she offers this stoic conclusion: "It's not such a bad way of getting through one's life."[32] From the point of view of her very Catholic piety, Sebastian's reception of this ritual ensures an eternity with God and renders the wretchedness of his short life ultimately inconsequential.

The Enchantment of a Sanctuary Lamp

Another sacred enchantment that inhabits Waugh's novel is that of the sanctuary lamp that burns in every Catholic church sanctuary. This light carries heavy symbolic weight in Waugh's novel. He describes this lamp in the family chapel at Brideshead as "a beaten-copper lamp of deplorable design."[33] Its flickering light within a red-tinted glass holder signals the presence of the Blessed Sacrament in the tabernacle. When the family chapel at Brideshead is shut down, the lamp is extinguished. Waugh describes the priest's ritual "decommissioning" of the chapel: the priest "emptied the holy water stoup and blew out the lamp in the sanctuary and left the tabernacle door open and empty, as though from now on it was always to be Good Friday."[34] For Waugh, the closing of this chapel with all its ritual detail serves as metaphor for the disenchantment descending over England in the first half of the twentieth century.

In the epilogue, Charles Ryder returns to Brideshead, which has escaped the destruction it had been marked for. He is surprised that the chapel has been reopened and the sanctuary lamp burns again, now serving soldiers who visit there in respite from their military exercises. In the chapel, the lifelong agnostic Charles kneels and says a prayer, "an ancient, newly learned form of words."[35]

Returning to his base, he muses on how Brideshead was built from the ruins of a European castle, how all great buildings develop and then decay. But this sense of futility, this vanity of vanities, is not the last word. Buildings always serve purposes the builders did not know of. So, too, this chapel with its sanctuary lamp burning again, symbol and reminder of all the lights that have served soldiers over the centuries. He realizes that the buildings of Brideshead, ancient yet surviving, are part of "the fierce little human tragedy in which I played a part."[36] The sanctuary lamp "could not have been lit but for the builders and the tragedians, and there I found it this morning, burning anew among the old stones."[37]

For Waugh, the homely sanctuary lamp with its easily extinguishable flame serves as a central symbol of God's enduring, if flickering, presence in the world. The novel moves through the faux enchantments of Sebastian and Charles's romance and Charles and Julia's affair to the genuine enchantment of God's saving presence symbolized in this ritual flame.

Outsiders and Failed Atheists

Waugh, a convert to the Catholic faith in a nation overwhelmingly Anglican, was eager to emphasize how Catholics were seen as outsiders in British society. Waugh's characters struggle to explain how and why Catholic families are so unlike other British. Catholics are "somehow set apart from their fellows, garlanded victims, devoted to the sacrifice."[38] They may try to fit in, but their beliefs and rituals constantly make them stand out as different.

We have seen how T. S. Eliot, the American transplant, and James Joyce saw themselves as outsiders. At midcentury, Flannery O'Connor will raise the stakes, insisting that Catholics are not only outliers in the surrounding culture but are, necessarily, misfits within a nonbelieving world.

In the first half of the twentieth century, Catholics felt themselves as outsiders in two ways: British Catholics were outsiders within a culture overwhelmingly Anglican, just as American Catholics early in the century would feel like outsiders in a nation still dominated by Protestants. And, at another level, British and American Catholics felt like outsiders in a historical period of disenchantment. To many in this century who had become disenchanted by two world wars and the ascendency of rationalism and science, religious faith was reduced to an outsider status.

The character of Charles Ryder will be the first of a stock character—the failed atheist—in Catholic novelists in the first half of the century. Astonished by the dysfunction of Sebastian's very Catholic family, Charles has been an atheist his whole life. His relationship with the Flyte family at Brideshead only confirmed his resistance to any religious belief. But this association, at the same time, draws him toward its belief system. As Charles watched Lord Marchmain approach his death, he found himself uttering a prayer for the old man. As the novel ends, he has entered the chapel at Brideshead, genuflected, blessed himself, and uttered a prayer. His atheism has not been able to withstand God's intrusion on his life. He ends a believer despite himself.

Graham Greene, in *The End of the Affair*, will create a character very much in this same guise. Novelist Walker Percy will follow suit, inventing a character who belongs to an extended family of Catholics yet resists the Faith. Only at the close of these novels do these men succumb to God's insistent advance. In the end, their well-defended atheism is no match for a demanding and ultimately merciful God. Waugh's novel pictures God as a threatening but redeeming force. Divine grace is both inscrutable and capricious. We only know that our being saved has nothing to do with our virtue. Waugh makes this point with his judgment about "the universal drama in which there is only one Actor."[39]

Afterthoughts

More than a decade after his novel had appeared, Waugh wrote, "When I wrote *Brideshead Revisited* I was consciously writing an obituary of the doomed English upper class."[40] Early in the novel, Waugh had linked the grand tradition of England with the rich heritage of the Catholic faith. The family history of the Flyte family, in all its eccentricities, "was typical of the Catholic squires of England."[41] But these grand families—both British and Christian—were perishing in the onslaught of modernity, represented by the planned replacement of estates like Brideshead with shopping centers.

In the preface to a subsequent novel, *The Sword of Honour*, published in 1964, Waugh observed that in this later novel, "I had written an obituary of the Roman Catholic Church in England as it had existed for many centuries."[42] These remarks were in the context of the

Second Vatican Council, just concluding. He detested the changes launched in the Council, saving his invective for the vernacular replacing Latin in the liturgy and the simplifying of earlier traditional devotions; these changes he described as "the buggering up of the Church [which] is a deep sorrow to me."[43] A year later, in an essay in the *Tablet* (August 21, 1965), he described the Council's effort to update the Latin liturgy as comparable to "throwing it in the gutter, or the sewer, of modern usage."[44]

Literary critic Ian Ker captures what was overthrown for Waugh in the Council: "That routine, even mechanical practice of Catholicism, that moral and canonical inflexibility, that cut-and-dried theology . . . were the very factors which had not only drawn Waugh to the order of the Church as against the chaos of the modern world, but contributed so significantly to the creation of some of the best novels of the twentieth century."[45] Waugh died on Easter Sunday in 1966, after participating in a traditional High Mass in Latin.

[1] Evelyn Waugh, *Brideshead Revisited*, 31.
[2] Waugh, 279.
[3] Waugh, 15.
[4] Waugh, 21.
[5] Waugh.
[6] Waugh, 23.
[7] Waugh.
[8] Waugh, 31.
[9] Waugh, 79.
[10] Waugh, 104.
[11] Waugh, 105.
[12] Waugh.
[13] Waugh.
[14] Waugh, 128.
[15] Waugh.
[16] Waugh, 169.
[17] Waugh, 226
[18] Waugh, 227
[19] Waugh.
[20] Waugh, 121.
[21] Waugh, 239.
[22] Waugh, 276.
[23] Waugh, 189.
[24] Waugh, 276
[25] Waugh, 279.
[26] Waugh, 340.
[27] Waugh,
[28] Waugh, 220.
[29] Waugh.
[30] Waugh, 338.
[31] Waugh, 259.
[32] Waugh, 309.
[33] Waugh, 351.
[34] Waugh, 220.
[35] Waugh, 350.
[36] Waugh, 351.
[37] Waugh.
[38] Waugh, 139.
[39] Waugh. 338.
[40] Waugh, *The Sword of Honor*, Preface, ix.
[41] Waugh, *Brideshead Revisited*, 139.
[42] Waugh, *The Sword of Honor*, Preface, ix.
[43] Ian Ker, *The Catholic Revival in English Literaure, 1845–61*, 202.
[44] Garry Wills, *The Future of the Catholic Church with Pope Francis*, 19.
[45] Ker, 202.

Chapter Three
We Could All Be Saints

℘

"I'll give him up forever, only let him be alive."

—Graham Greene, *The End of the Affair*

Graham Greene, in *The End of the Affair*, tells a story with four main characters: Maurice Bendrix, a novelist; his acquaintance Henry Miles, a midlevel civil servant; and Henry's wife, Sarah, with whom Bendrix will soon begin an affair. And we are alerted to a fourth, unseen, player who insinuates himself into the drama: an unnamed divine person that the atheist Bendrix "hated without yet knowing him."[1]

To gather material for a novel he is writing, Bendrix begins quizzing Sarah about her husband's work. "I had the cold-blooded intentions of picking the brain of a civil servant's wife."[2] Soon these friendly interrogations included lunch, with Bendrix still believing, "I had no idea whatever of falling in love with her."[3] Her wit and beauty placed her well out of his league. "I have always found it hard to feel sexual desire without some sense of superiority, mental or physical."[4] He was sure there would be no falling in love. But fall they did.

The unmarried Bendrix and married Sarah had had affairs before. Short-term affairs with no commitment suited them well: Bendrix needed the freedom to write, and Sarah still chose to stay in her marriage with Henry.

They knew just what they wanted; Sarah: "I want ordinary, corrupt human love."[5] The terms of the affair were clear: "We had agreed so happily to eliminate God from our world."[6] But the enchantment that ensued unsettled this hedged arrangement. They came to want more than an affair could produce, and these nonbelievers found they could not so easily eliminate the God who haunted their lives.

The affair between Maurice Bendrix and Sarah Miles began in 1939 and came to an end in June 1944 with the German bombing of London. When a bomb destroyed the building adjacent to Bendrix's apartment where they were making love, Bendrix left the bedroom to check the damage. Another bomb exploded, and he collapsed on the stairs with a door fallen on top of him. Sarah rushed naked from the room and saw Bendrix lying there, bloodied and apparently dead. Returning to the bedroom, she knelt and prayed: "Let him be alive, and I *will* believe. . . . I love him and I'll do anything if you'll make him alive. I said very slowly, I'll give him up forever, only let him be alive."[7]

At that point Bendrix, his pajamas bloodied, reentered the room, very much alive. So it seemed that God had answered her prayer. Seeing her kneeling, he asks what she was doing; and hearing that she, fellow nonbeliever, was praying, he wondered: Praying to what? Sarah answered, "To anything that might exist." She does not tell him of the bargain with God she has just consummated and abruptly leaves the room, dramatically ending the affair.

A year and a half later, Bendrix and Henry meet by chance and the affair between Bendrix and Henry's wife is again ignited. Knowing that she has broken her vow to end the adulterous affair, Sarah boldly proclaims, "I'm going to make him happy, that's my second vow, God, and stop me if you can, stop me if you can." But, of course, God can and does stop her. A severe cough— "it seemed too big a cough for her small body"—quickly turns into pneumonia and after a few weeks, she dies. In her final illness, Sarah comes to a belief in God and begins receiving instructions in preparation for entering the Catholic Church. As the novel ends, Bendrix, unrepentant, prays to God to leave him alone. "I found the one prayer that seemed to serve the winter mood: O God, You've done enough, You've robbed me of enough, I'm too tired and old to learn to love, leave me alone for ever."[8]

An Antagonistic God

Bendrix and Sarah share an attitude toward God that is a signature feature of Catholic devotion in the first half of the twentieth century. God is a divine intruder who disrupts their selfish lives; the God in whom they do not believe is antagonistic, adversarial, and relentless in the pursuit of souls.

Bendrix constantly battles with God, in whom he continues to insist he does not believe. "I hate you if you exist."[9] His relationship with this nonexistent God is a pugnacious one. When his affair with Sarah is rekindled, he mocks God, "I have won."[10] But finally the tables are turned. "You won in the end."[11]

Bendrix comes to see himself as a minor character in God's novel, a character that the Creator-author must flesh out for his own purposes. Bendrix feels like a character in the novel that will not come alive. An author like Bendrix might try to vivify the character but it resists, remaining pallid and unbelievable. Then the author (in this case, God) must make a special effort to bring this character (like Bendrix) alive because the plot cannot do without him. "We are inextricably bound to the plot, and wearily God forces us, here and there, according to his intention, characters without poetry, without free will, whose only importance is that somewhere, at some time, we help to furnish the scene in which a living character moves and speaks, providing perhaps the saints with the opportunities for their free will."[12] *"Wearily God forces us."*

Bendrix follows Sarah into a church, hoping to console and perhaps win her back. But Sarah will not be consoled; she leaves the church building and him with the remark, "God bless you." Bendrix, the nonbeliever, responds, "I repeated her blessing back to her." He reflects that he could now "imagine a God blessing her: or a God loving her."[13] Greene is telling the reader that Bendrix's wall of disbelief is beginning to crumble.

In his novel *The Heart of the Matter* (1948), Greene returns to this antagonistic image of God. The main character, Henry Scobie, has been persuaded by his wife to go to Mass and Communion with her, even though he is in sin from his adulterous affair. As he kneels to receive Communion (and so, committing a yet more egregious sin), "he saw only the priest's skirt like the skirt of the medieval war-horse bearing down upon him: the flapping of feet: the charge of God."[14] God the insistent, intruding, demanding judge.

As Scobie proceeds with his plans for suicide—escaping the dilemma of loving two women and a pointless career—he thinks of God. "As for God, he could speak to Him only as one speaks to an enemy—there was bitterness between them."[15]

A Materialistic Faith

In their happier days, Sarah and her husband, Henry, had taken a vacation in Spain where they visited an old church that was filled with garish, pious statues. When Sarah expressed her displeasure at such ugly art, Henry reminded her that the Catholic faith is materialistic. Greene intends to jar his readers with this observation. We often think of Christian faith as spiritual, which should mean beliefs that transcend the body and its physiological demands and corruptible flesh. To hear the Faith called "materialistic" can be shocking.

Earlier in the novel, Sarah had entered another Catholic church. Greene tells us of her reaction: "It was a Roman church, full of plaster statues and bad art, realistic art. I hated the statues, the crucifix, all the emphasis on the human body."[16] In her effort to end the affair, she wanted a more ethereal God, distant from the confusion of passionate bodies. Instead the church flaunted "the bodies standing around me on all the altars—the hideous plaster statues with the complacent faces, and I remembered that they believed in the resurrection of the body, the body I wanted destroyed forever."[17]

In *The Heart of the Matter*, Greene returns to this "bad art" concern. The main character, Scobie, looks around in a Catholic church at "the plaster statues with the swords in the bleeding hearts" and "the plaster Virgin, the hideous stations [of the Cross]."[18] Both Waugh and Greene were no doubt aware of the critical judgments of non-Catholics about this pietistic art. Waugh had described the sanctuary lamp that plays such an important role in his novel as "a beaten-copper lamp of deplorable design."[19] Each brings to their descriptions another point as well: tasteless, ugly art only emphasizes that God's grace is not dependent on human-made beauty.

Greene is reminding the reader that the Catholic faith is an incarnational faith: rooted in the physical body with all its awkwardness and vulnerability. The faith is rooted in Jesus as a real, embodied individual in whom God resides. The sacraments—of Baptism, Eucharist, Anointing—depend on the physical elements of water, bread, oil. Greene's very Catholic point is that human "materialistic" bodies are not obstacles to spiritual belief, but the fragile portals, the essential media for faith.

As lust gives way to love, Sarah recognizes that she now wants much more than the "ordinary corrupt human love"[20] that once seemed sufficient. Now she pictures the body of her lover surviving beyond death. Such a body would have to still bear the marks of its corruptible flesh. If her love for Bendrix might survive their deaths, she would want the scar on his shoulder to be there for her to touch and kiss. Greene's insistence on Christian faith as "materialistic" is intimately linked to the novel's celebration of touch.

We Could All Be Saints

The ideal of sainthood stands out in many of the Catholic novels of the first half of the twentieth century. In *Brideshead Revisited*, Waugh describes Sebastian's mother: "Mummy is popularly believed to be a saint."[21] In Greene's *The End of the Affair*, Bendrix grieves his loss of Sarah and acknowledges that she has taken a leap of faith. "If this God exists, I thought, and if even you—with your lusts and adulteries and the timid lies you used to tell—can change like this, *we could all be saints* by leaping as you lept, by shutting the eyes and leaping once and for all."[22] In Greene's *The Power and the Glory*, the whisky priest is sure that, in his sinfulness, he is in no way saintly. Yet on his "wanted" poster in a police station, someone has drawn a halo around his head. And his execution makes him a martyr and, by definition, a saint. Greene sums up this ongoing theme in the novel: the whisky priest "knew now that at the end there was only one thing that counted—to be a saint."[23]

Thomas Merton reported in *The Seven Storey Mountain* an exchange that continued this romance of sainthood. His friend Robert Lax asked Merton, two years before he was to enter the Trappists, what he aspired to become. Merton's first response named his ambition to become a famous writer. Lax objected: "'What you should say,'—he told me—'what you should say is that you want to be a saint.'"[24] Dorothy Day will redirect this ideal of personal holiness in a social direction with her demand, "Where are the saints to try to change the social order?"[25]

With the sea change of Vatican II in the 1960s, the ideal of becoming exceptionally holy, often apart from engagement in the broader world, began to be replaced by an enthusiasm for becoming fully human. Mary Gordon and Marilynne Robinson will focus their novelistic themes on what Robinson calls "the rituals of the ordinary."[26] A recovery of a Christian humanism with its ideal of human flourishing guides this turn in the Catholic imagination. Scholars joined novelists to encourage this shift: art historian Hans Rookmaaker writes, "Christ didn't come to make us Christians. He came to make us fully human."[27]

The Grace of Touch

Bendrix recalls his first impression of Sarah: "All I noticed about her that first time was her beauty and her happiness and her way of touching people with her hands as though she loved them."[28] The novel will turn, again and again, to the power of touch in every kind of loving.

After their affair had ended, Bendrix follows Sarah into a church where she sits crying in a pew. Desperate to console her, he puts his hand on her knee. "If only one had a touch that could heal."[29] Greene is alluding here to gospel memories of Jesus touching the ill to effect healing. In Mark's gospel, Jesus almost needs to touch others, make physical contact, for this healing to take place. In Luke's gospel, we read that many ill persons were brought to Jesus and "he laid his hands on each of them and cured them" (Luke 4:40). In one striking instance, an ill woman approaches and touches

Jesus's cloak, and it is her courageous touch that initiates healing (Luke 8:46). And, of course, in the Catholic heritage the sacraments are gestures of touch: pouring water in Baptism; consecrated bread going from hand to hand; a minister's touch, with cooling oil, to the forehead of a fevered patient.

Sarah, writing in her journal, reminds God that even her adulterous touching of Bendrix opened some part of her heart that has led to her being in touch with God. "Could I have touched You if I hadn't touched him first, touched him as I never touched Henry, anybody?" This theme of the sensual as portal to the sacred will come into full view in novelists later in the century.

After Sarah repents of her adulterous ways and takes the leap of faith, Greene inserts two miraculous touches into the story. Sarah had been seeing a Mr. Smythe, a rationalist philosopher from whom she had sought counsel after hearing him preach in the public park against religion. Paradoxically, his arguments had brought Sarah to belief and she had determined to seek instruction in the Catholic faith. Mr. Smythe has a disfigured cheek, and after seeing him for the last time, Sarah kisses him on it: "I shut my eyes and put my mouth against the cheek. I felt sick for a moment because I fear deformity, and he sat quiet and let me kiss him."[30] After Sarah's death, Mr. Smythe feels obliged to tell Bendrix that her touch had healed his cheek.

The second incident concerned the young son of Mr. Parkis, who had been hired by Henry as an investigator to determine if Sarah was having an affair with anyone. His young son had a serious stomach problem, and again, after Sarah's death, the boy has a dream of her coming to touch his stomach. The boy "told the doctor it was Mrs. Miles [Sarah] who came and took away the pain—touching him on the right side of the stomach if you'll forgive the indelicacy."[31]

As the novel comes to a close, Sarah has died and Bendrix is now staying with Henry. One night as they prepare to head to the pub for their evening beers, Bendrix helps Henry with his shoelace, then brushes some dust off his shoulder, and, as they leave the house, "I put my hand on Henry's arm and held it there; I had to be strong for both of us now." The novel ends with this final gesture—Bendrix touching Henry with compassion. This contact, non-erotic and non-romantic, announces yet another healing power of touch.

Human touch, sometimes mere physical contact, at times manipulative, even destructive, retains the potential to calm and console, to arouse. As parents and lovers know, touch can be most enchanting.

The "Ends" of the Affair

The heart of Greene's novel is the bombing that interrupts the lovers' tryst and Sarah's promise to leave Bendrix if God will grant him life. Sarah's vow marks the first "end" of their affair. But there will be yet more terminations.

The second ending takes place after the two had begun their affair again. Sarah repents and leaves Bendrix. A more striking "ending" occurs as the couple's erotic delights are unintentionally transformed from lust to love. Lust—the temporary, mutual use of each other's body for pleasure—had at first satisfied their expectations of the affair. They wanted nothing more complicating than this temporary faux enchantment. Sarah intended to remain in her marriage. Bendrix had had many affairs and was absorbed in his own career. The two of them seemed to enter this relationship with no strings attached. But the affair became more than either had planned. They began to fall in love, and this genuine enchantment doomed their ability to meet at a mere superficial exchange of lust.

Greene has crafted a novel that describes the dangers of falling in love. Affairs fit a disenchanted world: moments of temporary delight in a world that offers nothing richer. But a couple may fall, accidentally, in love and begin yearning for more from one another. The enchantment of genuine love—which asks and expects everything—renders an affair deeply unsatisfying. After their affair has ended the first time, Bendrix is tempted to begin another affair to fill the empty space in his heart. But he finds, sitting with an attractive young woman, "I felt no desire for her at all. It was as if quite suddenly after all the promiscuous years I had grown up. My passion for Sarah had killed simple lust for ever. Never again would I be able to enjoy a woman without love."[32] The affair ended when genuine love intruded.

The ultimate ending of the affair takes place with Sarah's death. Bendrix is broken by the turn of events: he is bereft of both lust and love. Greene clumsily inserts an explanation that Sarah had been baptized Catholic as a child and so was, despite herself, a Christian all her life. In the novel she is portrayed as saintly now; her sudden cold that led to pneumonia and her death was fitting punishment for her infidelity.

Afterthoughts

Greene became a Catholic in 1926 when marrying his wife, Vivien. He described himself as "keeping one foot in the Church" and was acutely aware of the tension between religious doctrine and the imaginative freedom demanded of a novelist, and he warned that the novelist must resist the warm embrace of a church that will easily transform loyalty to its orthodoxy into a vice that will cripple a novelist.

In 1948, Greene spoke on BBC radio about the influence of his Catholic faith on his writing: "I belong to a group, the Catholic Church, which would present me with grave problems as a writer if I were not saved by my disloyalty."[33] He adds, "If only writers could maintain that one virtue—so much more important to them than purity—unspotted from the world. Honours, State patronage, success, the praise of their fellows all tend to sap their disloyalty. If they don't become loyal to a Church or a country, they are too apt to become loyal to some invented ideology of their own. . . . Given time the writer will be corrupted into loyalty."[34]

Equating loyalty with slavish conformity, Greene concludes, "Loyalty confines us to accepted opinions: loyalty forbids us to comprehend sympathetically our dissident fellows; but disloyalty encourages us to roam experimentally through any human mind; it gives to the novelist the extra dimension of sympathy."[35] Flannery O'Connor's caustic evaluation of pietistic writing fits Greene's meaning of *loyalty:* "When the Catholic novelist closes his eyes and tries to see with the eyes of the Church, the result is another addition to that large body of pious trash for which we have for so long been famous."[36]

A defining image of Greene's posture of "one foot in the Church" was the photo that appeared in newspapers of his funeral with two lovely older women, dressed in funereal black, standing side by side: his wife and his mistress.

[1] Graham Greene, *The End of the Affair,* 36.

[2] Greene, *The End of the Affair,* 10.

[3] Greene, *The End of the Affair,* 25.

[4] Greene.

[5] Greene, 89.

[6] Greene, 69

[7] Greene, 95.

[8] Greene, 192.

[9] Greene, 136.

[10] Greene, 165.

[11] Greene, 165.

[12] Greene, 186.

[13] Greene, 131.

[14] Graham Greene, *The Heart of the Matter,* 209.

[15] Greene, 219.

[16] Greene, *The End of the Affair,* 109.

[17] Greene.

[18] Greene, *The Heart of the Matter,* 205.

[19] Evelyn Waugh, *Brideshead Revisited,* 351.

[20] Greene, *The End of the Affair,* 89, 124.

[21] Waugh, *Brideshead Revisited,* 89.

[22] Greene, *The End of the Affair,* 190. Emphasis added.

[23] Graham Greene, *The Power and the Glory,* 210.

[24] Thomas Merton, *The Seven Storey Mountain,* 260.

[25] Dorothy Day, *Selected Writings,* xii.

[26] Marilynne Robinson, *Housekeeping,* 16.

[27] Gregory Wolfe, *Beauty Will Save the World,* 46.

[28] Greene, 25.

[29] Greene, 128.

[30] Greene, 122.

[31] Greene, 178.

[32] Greene, 58.

[33] Richard Greene, *Graham Greene: A Life in Letters,* 151.

[34] Richard Greene, 154–55.

[35] Richard Greene, 155.

[36] Flannery O'Connor, *Mystery and Manners,* 180.

Chapter Four
Catholic Enchantment:
French Accents

*"To light up the secret sources of sanctity in creatures which
seem to us to have failed."*

—François Mauriac's definition of the novel

At mid-century, two French Catholic writers began to
gain the attention of Catholics in the United States.
In 1951, the film version of Georges Bernanos' novel
The Diary of a Country Priest acquainted many Americans for the first time with this quintessential Catholic
novel. In 1952, the French Catholic novelist François
Mauriac was awarded the Nobel Prize for Literature.
Subsequently, his novel *Viper's Tangle* (1933) found
an expanded readership in the US. Like Waugh and
Greene, Mauriac describes characters who hold out, if
unsuccessfully, against God's intrusive grace.

George Bernanos: *The Diary of a Country Priest*

In his 1937 prize-winning novel, Georges Bernanos
recounts the life of a simple pastor in a rural parish in
France. The story gives a glimpse into Catholic beliefs at
this time, beliefs that would be retraced a decade later
in Evelyn Waugh's *Brideshead Revisited*. When the novel

was made into an acclaimed film by Robert Bresson in 1951, it would impress American Catholic writers Thomas Merton, Dorothy Day, and Flannery O'Connor.

Bernanos sounds the theme of disenchantment in the first pages of the novel. "My parish is bored stiff; no other word for it. . . . We can see them being eaten up by boredom and we can't do anything about it."[1] The priest, left nameless in the novel, then describes this boredom as "an aborted despair, shameful form of despair in some way like the fermentation of a Christianity in decay."[2]

The local parish priest who is writing this diary is of humble stock. Bernanos portrays him as a social misfit. His tattered cassock makes him a laughing stock of those he meets. Even schoolgirls laugh at him. The priest is in the world, but not of it. He has received a poor education at his seminary and repeatedly tells the reader of his social awkwardness, his ignorance and general ineptness in his daily ministry. He accuses himself—one of numerous self-indictments—of lack of compassion.

As he goes about his ministry, he is visited by various senior clergy who encourage him to accommodate himself to the times, not try to do too much. His mentor, M. le Curé de Torcy, so encourages him, as does the regional dean who accuses the poor priest of assuming the airs of "an intellectual" or, worse, a poet. The dean counsels, "Work will put you right."[3]

If the world of this novel is a wretched place, poor and boring and its priests largely inept, it doesn't greatly matter since God loves the world and will save its people despite themselves. Bernanos' priest reminds the reader that we can expect little from the world or even from the Church; we are saved by God's grace, apart from the futile efforts of priests like him.

The Enchanting Workings of Grace

As the diary unfolds, we watch this priest go through his daily rounds in the small town of Ambricourt, celebrating Mass and visiting the ill and dying. He refers again and again to his own inadequacy. He is not only poor—financially and in terms of talent—but becomes increasingly ill. He is plagued by headaches and a severely upset stomach. He is reduced to taking only "bread and wine" as his meager sustenance. This unhappy tale is broken only by a set piece at the center of the novel involving the family that occupies the one chateau within his parish boundaries. The head of the chateau, M. le Comte, is an unfaithful spouse who spends his time shooting rabbits and insulting the socially inferior priest. His wife, Mme la Comtesse, is engulfed in chronic grief over the death at eighteen months of her only son. Their teenage daughter, Mlle Chantal, converts her own grief and confusion into hateful behavior toward her mother.

When the parish priest visits the chateau to speak with the mother, she expresses her anger at her daughter who, she feels, has bonded with her husband and shut her out, leaving her to suffer alone the loss of her son. The priest, despite his many early protestations of ineptness, suddenly displays great skill in confronting the woman. When the woman persists in outrage at her daughter, the priest parries her every effort to defend her toxic attitude. He reminds her that hell is the absence of love—an absence she is chronically exhibiting—and should she die now, she would be unable to be with her son in heaven. Finally, she breaks down, acknowledging the grief that has fueled her bitterness. "I have willfully sinned against hope."[3] The priest gently accepts this informal confession, and the scene concludes with her repentance before God and the priest. She assures the priest that she will go the next day to receive the Sacrament of Confession from her usual confessor.

That evening, after writing a letter of gratitude to the priest, she suddenly dies of a heart attack. Bernanos is reminding readers that the woman's formal confession intended for the next day is, ultimately, not important. The repentance and grace of forgiveness had already taken place the day before, through the efforts of the visiting priest. When the priest returns to the chateau, he looks at the peaceful expression on the deceased woman's face and wonders, "Oh, miracle—thus to be able to give what we ourselves do not possess, sweet miracle of our empty hands."[4] Here lies Bernanos' central theme: God's grace works its saving wonders through poor, inadequate human beings such as the priest. For Bernanos, this is the enchantment of grace.

A quick read of the novel might suggest that the priest's counseling skills had brought the woman to her change of heart. But Bernanos made clear that pastoral skills of the priest are not relevant here. The priest is keenly aware that, ungifted though he be, God has seen fit to act—relying not on his ministerial skills but his mere presence to the woman—to break open and heal the woman's heart. So the priest exclaims, "Sweet miracle of our empty hands!"[5] God's grace has moved through his empty hands to work this transformation.

Experienced therapists acknowledge such mysterious events as part of their calling: a troubled individual pours out his heart in the presence of a counselor; with little intervention by the therapist, the person comes to a healing insight about some part of his life. The counselor's attentive presence was the occasion of the healing insight, but his skills were not the cause. The mysteriousness of such healing, and the consolation it affords both persons, only confirms the therapist's calling. A Christian counselor will name this surprising transformation grace. God's grace has not descended miraculously from *beyond* human life; instead it has stirred *within* the human relationship, though in ways neither person fully comprehends. For those with the eyes to see, this is both grace and enchantment.

In the final chapter of the novel, Bernanos returns to this central theme. The priest's illness has progressed and been diagnosed as incurable stomach cancer. In his last days, he goes to visit an old friend from seminary days, a person who has since left the priesthood. When he learns that the local parish priest cannot come to administer the Last Rites, he asks his old friend, the ex-priest, for absolution. Though no longer an officially recognized priest, his friend reluctantly agrees to perform the sacramental rite of forgiveness and blessing. This "irregular" administration of the sacrament by someone no longer a priest in good standing will suffice. Bernanos is reminding readers that God's grace does not wait upon the official ministrations of Church personnel. God moves mysteriously but effectively through untalented pastors and de-frocked priests. Bernanos has the dying priest utter as his last words, "It doesn't matter. All is grace."[5]

Twice in the novel Bernanos evokes the Catholic belief in the communion of saints. This is the belief, repeated each Sunday in the Apostles' Creed ("I believe in the communion of saints, the forgiveness of sins . . . ") that pictures a mystical unity of all believers, saints and sinners, as they move together toward a final gathering in God. In Bernanos, the priest asks a troubled woman, "Don't you ever despair?"[6] Instead of despair, the woman, in her suffering, identifies with all those in the world who are also suffering, many whose circumstances are more difficult than her own.

"I think of all the people I don't know of like me—an' there's plenty of 'em, a wide world it is—beggars ploddin' through the rain, kiddies with no home, all the ailin' and the mad folk in the asylums cryin' to the moon, and plenty, plenty more."[7] Placing herself with this ensemble of sufferers, she tells the priest that the voices of this multitude across history come to her "like a great murmurin' sendin' me to sleep."[8] The sense of solidarity that describes the communion of saints brings with it a consolation that permits rest in the midst of suffering.

Later, when the priest receives the diagnosis of his terminal cancer, the news does not isolate him or fill him with self-pity. He reminds himself of the many who are living out similar scenarios. "This very day hundreds, thousands of us perhaps, all over the world, will be dazed by a similar sentence."[9] In the midst of this bad news, he feels the consolation of being part of such a gathering.

For the priest, this spiritual belonging brings with it a sense of resilience. "But experience has also taught me that I have inherited from my mother, and no doubt from other poor women of our kind, a sort of endurance, which in the long run is almost unlimited, because it doesn't attempt to vie with pain, but slips within, makes of it a habit in some way; that is our strength."[10]

The novel comes to its climax with the priest's words: "Well, it's all over now. The strange mistrust I had of myself, of my own being, has flown. . . . I am reconciled to myself, to the poor, poor shell of me."[11] He consoles himself with the realization that "if pride could die in us, the supreme grace would be to love oneself in all simplicity—as one would love any one of those who themselves have suffered and loved in Christ."[12]

François Mauriac's *Viper's Tangle*

*"I suddenly had an intense feeling, an almost physical
certitude, that another world existed,
a reality of which we know nothing but the shadow."*

Monsieur Louis in *Viper's Tangle*

At the beginning of his novel, Mauriac inserts a "note to the reader," encouraging a compassionate response to the hateful but suffering main character. And he telegraphs the point of the novel: "All through his somber life, dark passions hide from him the light quite near at hand, of which a gleam, sometimes, falls upon him and is on the point of setting him afire—his own passions."[13]

The first half of this novel is a tirade of resentment by sixty-eight-year-old Monsieur Louis against his wife. Married for forty-five years, he believes her family has always looked down on him because of his peasant roots. He refers to "the great silence"[14] between them over four decades, after she confessed that she had loved another man before him. Once their three children were born, his wife focused all her energy on mothering, while he occupied himself with making money and the occasional affair. The old man wallows in his disappointment in love and his bitterness.

Mauriac situates the activity of the novel during Holy Week and records the old man ostentatiously eating meat on Fridays to flaunt his own nonbelief in his family's Catholicism. In his resentment, Louis is planning to cut out his wife and two surviving, ungrateful children from any inheritance. (His favorite child, Marie, had died in childhood from a sudden illness, and he was blamed by his wife for not calling a doctor soon enough.)

Yet the old man does recall a brief period of enchantment early in their marriage. Being very much in love, "I suddenly had an intense feeling, an almost physical certitude, that another world existed, a reality of which we know nothing but the shadow. . . ."[15] But that brief ecstatic state was long vanished, and he returns again and again to the despair that continues to occupy his heart. "You cannot imagine such a torture as this: to have had nothing out of life, and to await nothing after death—and to feel that there may be nothing beyond this world, that no explanation exists, that the word of the enigma will be given us."[16] Part One ends with his description of his sinful heart as "this tangle of vipers."[17] He judges it is impossible to separate these poisonous snakes except with a sword—a reference to the words of Scripture: "I have not come to bring peace, but a sword" (Matthew 10:34).

Cutting through the Viper's Tangle

Monsieur Louis suggests to his wife that God may not have come for the righteous like herself, but for sinners, like himself. And he becomes aware that his one spiritual lifeline is his love for his favorite child, the now-deceased Marie. He begins to experience the first stirrings of a reconciliation with his alienated wife. And he senses a new and surprising detachment from his former hatred and wonders, "What force is drawing me? A blind force? Love? Perhaps love."[18]

When his wife dies before him and he speaks with his once-alienated children, he feels a change in himself. "At that moment, I realized that my hatred was dead—and my desire for revenge was dead with it. It had been dead, perhaps, for a long time."[19] He suddenly feels detached from the fortune that he had clung to for so long. He is now willing to give the fortune to his children.

As he anticipates a reconciliation with his children, Louis muses, "I would pass through everything that had separated us. The tangle of vipers was at last cut through."[20] Monsieur Louis prays, "I seek Him Who alone can achieve that victory; and He must Himself be the Heart of hearts, the burning center of all love."[21]

In the final pages of the novel, the old man dies. Mauriac concludes the text with a letter from a granddaughter to her relatives; in it she writes that she is convinced that the old man had returned to the faith in his heart. She remembers that he had talked three times with the parish priest and intended to go to Confession and receive the sacrament before the coming Christmas

Mass. She admits that he was, in many ways, a dreadful person, but "that does not alter the fact that a great light shone upon him in his last days."[22]

Mauriac's novel belongs very much to the Catholic imagination that reigned in the first half of the century. A greedy, bitter man returns to the Catholic faith, somewhat miraculously, at the end of his life, saved by God's grace. Here as in Bernanos, the miracle of grace is presented as an enchantment: a surprising, unexplainable gift of new life. The old man here, like the main characters in Waugh's *Brideshead Revisited* and Greene's *The End of the Affair*, is a failed atheist.

Monsieur Louis in *Viper's Tangle* illustrates Mauriac's definition of the Catholic novel: "If there is a reason for the existence of the novelist on earth it is this: to show the element which holds out against God in the highest and noblest characters—the innermost evils and dissimulations; and also to light up the secret sources of sanctity in creatures which seem to us to have failed."[23]

Afterthoughts

Georges Bernanos (1888–1948) served in the First World War, and after the war he worked in the insurance business before writing *Sous le soleil de Satan* (1926; *Under the Sun of Satan*). He won the Grand Prix du roman de l'Académie française for *The Diary of a Country Priest* (*Journal d'un curé de campagne*), published in 1936. Like many French Catholics of this time, he was initially attracted to the *Action Française* and the rule of Franco in Spain before distancing himself from these far-right Catholic adventures. He complained about France's "spiritual exhaustion," which he saw as the cause of its collapse in 1940. After liberation, Bernanos returned to France from Brazil. But seeing no signs of a spiritual renewal in his country, he did not participate actively in French political life.

François Mauriac (1885–1970), member of the Académie française, won the Nobel Prize in Literature in 1952. He was awarded the Grand Cross of the *Légion d'honneur* in 1958.

Mauriac's influence on American Catholics extended well beyond his novels. In her 1938 memoir, *From Union Square to Rome*, Dorothy Day quoted a long passage from Mauriac that expressed his—and her—vision: "Jesus is disguised and masked in the midst of men, hidden among the poor, among the sick, among prisoners, among strangers."[24] Mauriac published an article, "The Final Answer," in *The Saturday Evening Post* (December 3, 1959) that served as a memoir, reflecting back on his own journey of faith. A colleague of ours reports that this essay contributed profoundly to his own decision to enter the Catholic Church.

1   Georges Bernanos, *The Diary of a Country Priest*, 1.
2   Bernanos, 3.
3   Bernanos, 175.
4   Bernanos, 180.
5   Bernanos, 298.
6   Bernanos, 289.
7   Bernanos.
8   Bernanos.
9   Bernanos, 260.
10 Bernanos.
11 Bernanos, 296.
12 Bernanos.
13 François Mauriac, *The Viper's Tangle*, 6.
14 Mauriac, 67.
15 Mauriac, 44.
16 Mauriac, 147.
17 Mauriac.
18 Mauriac, 149.
19 Mauriac, 272.
20 Mauriac, 247.
21 Mauriac, 251.
22 Mauriac, 280.
23 McInerny, 92.
24 Dorothy Day, *Selected Writings*, 6.

Part Two

❧

A Mid-Century Pivot in American Catholic Faith

At midcentury, American Catholics were reading Thomas Merton's *The Seven Storey Mountain*, Evelyn Waugh's *Brideshead Revisited*, and Graham Greene's *The End of the Affair*. Soon they would be able to appreciate Dorothy Day's memoir, *The Long Loneliness*, Flannery O'Connor's short stories, and Walker Percy's *The Moviegoer.*

The 1950s marked a sea change in Catholic faith and literature. Catholics were finding their voice and shedding their immigrant and outsider status in a culture that had been emphatically Protestant.

In these years, Thomas Merton and Dorothy Day were focusing their writing on an active engagement with the broader culture. At the same time, Flannery O'Connor and Walker Percy continued to address the disenchantment that still seemed to pervade American society.

During this same fertile decade, the writings of two French Catholic authors—Jacques Maritain and Pierre Teilhard de Chardin—began to attract the attention of American Catholics. Maritain's Christian humanism and Teilhard's vision of a cosmic evolution enchanted many of these Catholics.

Chapter Five
All My Life I Have Been
Haunted by God

*"The Church in America is largely an immigrant Church.
Culturally it is not on its feet, but it will get there."*

—Flannery O'Connor

In 1951, the Catholic presence in American culture suddenly turned up the volume. Bishop Fulton J. Sheen, resplendent in his red episcopal robes, cast his telegenic figure into the homes of millions of Catholics in his new TV show. This was something to be proud of. That same year, a brash twenty-six-year-old Catholic published the book, *God and Man at Yale*. In it, William F. Buckley Jr. proclaimed his arrival on the cultural scene with his *I am Catholic; hear me roar!* Less dramatically, the Jesuit scholar John Courtney Murray was lecturing that year at Yale University, honing his later contribution at Vatican II on religious freedom. The French Catholic philosopher Jacques Maritain was lecturing on Thomas Aquinas the same year at Princeton University, yet another Catholic intellectual teaching in a non-Catholic institution.

The following year was a bonanza for Catholic publishing. The French Catholic novelist François Mauriac was awarded the Nobel Prize for Literature. Dorothy Day published her memoir, *The Long Loneliness*, and

Flannery O'Connor saw her first novel, *Wise Blood*, into print. Meanwhile Thomas Merton's *The Seven Storey Mountain* continued to be a literary bestseller. The book in its first year (1948–49) had sold six hundred thousand copies, but *The New York Times* initially chose not to include it in its bestseller list, deeming it "a religious book."

Thomas Merton and Dorothy Day stand as pivotal authors in the shift in the Catholic imagination that was emerging at midcentury. When Merton turned his attention to social structures after a decade in the Trappist monastery, Dorothy Day had already been spending herself in challenging these structures for a quarter century. In the course of the 1950s and 1960s, they would together foster a new direction for Catholic faith: a more socially engaged and optimistic orientation. Dorothy Day's focus on happiness and life in abundance, even for the marginal in society, announced a new emphasis for the Catholic imagination.

Catholics in the 1950s

As the 1950s began, American Catholics stood on the cusp of a new era. Returning soldiers—offspring of Italian, Irish, and Polish immigrants—were entering college in large numbers, the first of their families to seek higher education. The next generation would continue this upward social mobility as Catholics replaced their outsider status for that of engaged citizens.

The 1950s represented the final decade in which American Catholics would abide in a sheltered existence, at arm's length from the culture and the world. Flannery O'Connor judged that "the Catholic in this country suffers from a parochial aesthetic and a cultural insularity."[1] During this decade, many American Catholics continued to live contentedly in their own insular neighborhoods. They often preferred to remain in areas with their own churches, schools and hospitals. Mary Gordon, in her novel *Final Payments*, has Isabel describe her own father's contentment. "It was natural for him not to want to leave the neighborhood where the church was so predominant it did not need to be upheld."[2] Catholics were aware that they belonged to the *Church Militant* and savored this posture in the hymn *Faith of Our Fathers*—"living still in spite of dungeon, fire and sword."

Catholics at midcentury were formed in a faith defined by the questions and answers in the Baltimore Catechism. The Legion of Decency made clear which films were acceptable, which condemned. Many families, including ours, posted this list on the refrigerator as a reminder. For those with more scholarly interests, the Index of Forbidden Books still prevailed. Catholic rhetoric was harsh in its warning about the perils of association with non-Catholics. Flannery O'Connor defended her use of misfits and freaks in her short stories: writers "must often tell 'perverse' stories to 'shock' a morally blind world."[3] Evelyn Waugh had described his intent in writing *Brideshead Revisited*: "to trace the divine purpose in a pagan world."[4]

In Mary Gordon's *Final Payments*, Isabel remembers her religious education during that decade: the nuns insisted that the girls, when going to Communion, would "fold our hands so that they were Gothic steeples, not a mess of immigrant knuckles." The pious

gesture of folded hands in church had a cultural com-
ponent: distancing the girls from their immigrant roots.
Isabel's father, a devout Catholic steeped in this tradition, "believed in hierarchies; he believed that truth
and beauty could be achieved only by a process of
chastening and exclusion. One did not look for happiness on earth; there was a glory in poverty."[5] This
turn away from the world, an embrace of one's outsider status, and a renunciation of earthly happiness
describe the Catholic imagination that still reigned
at midcentury.

Catholic identity was clear and exclusive: clear in
doctrine and devotion; exclusive as Catholics separated themselves from the surrounding environment
of "non-Catholics." Graham Greene had described "the
hard edges of Catholicism" that gave a satisfying clarity
and confidence in the midst of the upheavals and turmoil in the world. Gordon caught this edge in *Final Payments*: "Protestants, it said, thought about moral issues,
drank water and ate crackers, took care to exercise and
had a notion that charity was synonymous with good
works. Catholics, on the other hand, thought about
eternity, drank wine and smoked cigars, were sometimes extravagant, but knew that charity was a fire in
the heart of God and never confused it with the Protestant invention, philanthropy."[6]

In his account of this period, Paul Elie notes the
peculiar location of Catholics in the broader culture. In Europe, it had been Protestant Christians
who stood out in a largely Catholic culture such as
that of France or Spain. Now, in the United States,
"it was the Catholics who stood apart. Even as they

made their way into society, as shopkeepers and laborers, police officers and politicians, they were taught to cherish separateness as a virtue, the worldly expression of the virtue of purity sought in convents and monasteries."[7]

The reign of Pope Pius XII from 1939 to 1958 provided a fitting symbol of this style of Catholicism. The papacy was still smarting from its loss of the Papal States as Italy consolidated its national identity. Pius XII was often described as "a prisoner of Vatican"—that shrunken territory that remained from more glorious days. He never traveled beyond this domain; when he did appear in public, he wore a crown that was reminiscent of a medieval prince and was carried on a palanquin resting on the shoulders of attendants. When the pope died at the end of the decade, the cardinals elected an aged member of their ranks to carry on this style of leadership. To their great surprise, the seventy-six-year-old successor to Pius XII, John XXIII, almost immediately called for a worldwide council that would wrest the Church from its insular, defensive posture and bring it into an enthusiastic engagement with the broader culture.

The decade of the 1950s represented the culmination of one Catholic imagination—witnessed to in the novels of Waugh, Greene, Mauriac, and even Flannery O'Connor. During these same years, new energies and ideals emerged that would soon shift the focus from that of outsiders to that of engaged citizens and from an individualistic piety to a collective devotion. We see this transition most dramatically in the evolving vocation of Thomas Merton.

The Monkish Merton: Exile in a "Stupid and Godless Society"

In 1941, a twenty-seven-year-old failed novelist decided to forsake the world and enter the solitude of a Trappist monastery. In his best-selling memoir, *The Seven Storey Mountain* (published in 1948), Thomas Merton wrote of his longing for a community of believers "who had banded themselves together to form a small, secret colony of the Kingdom of Heaven in this earth of exile."[8]

In his introduction to the book, Robert Giroux, Merton's editor, judged that its surprising popularity may have been due to the mood of disillusionment that was pervasive in the United States in the late 1940s. With the end of World War II, the Cold War had commenced and people were looking for reassurance. Merton's memoir stood, like Waugh's *Brideshead Revisited* (1945) and Graham Greene's *The End of the Affair* (1951), as a story of religious enchantment within a disenchanted world.

Merton begins his memoir in a style reminiscent of Augustine's *Confessions,* castigating himself and denouncing the world. He tells the reader that he was "prisoner of my own violence and my own selfishness, in the image of the world into which I was born. That world was the picture of Hell."[9] And he salts his story with condemnations of all that is not Catholic, referring to "the sterility and inefficacy of Anglicanism in the moral order. . ."[10] and to "French charity [that had lapsed] into a disgusting, fleshy concupiscence."[11]

Merton writes of his motive for entering the monastery: to "learn from God how to be happy"[12] which will demand learning to hate himself. "The most effective way of detaching us from ourselves is to make us detest ourselves as we have made ourselves by sin."[13] He warns his readers: a person must become alert to "your enemies, the devil and your own imagination and the inherent vulgarity of your own corrupted nature [that] can get at you."[14]

"A Garden That Was Dead and Stripped and Bare."

Merton turned to the biblical imagery of a garden to describe his entry into the monastery. He was, of course, attuned to the garden of Eden where Adam and Eve first flourished—an idyllic place from which they would soon be exiled. And he was likely aware of Evelyn Waugh's *Brideshead Revisited*, which had been published in 1945 while he was composing his own memoir. In Waugh's novel, Charles Ryder's fascination with Sebastian Flyte (and all things Catholic) was pictured as an entry into an "enclosed and enchanted garden."[15]

Merton describes that fateful day in December 1941: "Brother Matthew locked the gate behind me and I was enclosed in the four walls of my new freedom. And it was appropriate that the beginning of freedom should be as it was. For I entered a garden that was dead and stripped and bare."[16] Merton savors the paradox of a barren, wintry garden as the place where he would seek and find his spiritual enchantment.

In the years after entering the monastery, Merton's attention began to shift from a world-rejecting asceticism to a concern for the world beyond the sanctuary of his monastic life. In *Seeds of Contemplation* (published in 1949, the year after *The Seven-Storey Mountain*), we hear the first stirrings of a new concern about isolating himself from humanity. During these same years, he was certainly watching from within the monastery walls the social activism of Dorothy Day as she protested the war, joined union boycotts, and cared for the poor and disenfranchised of the world.

Several years into the 1950s, Merton began to publish articles in the new Catholic magazine, *Jubilee*, first published in 1953, which illustrated this new focus. Merton now forcefully supported a just-emerging view of Catholic liturgy: less about personal devotion and more about a worship that is engaged with a suffering world. Now Merton would insist that "Our life in Christ, therefore, calls for a fully Eucharistic apostolate—a far-seeing and energetic action, based on prayer and interior union with God, which is able to transcend the limitations of class and nation and culture and continue to build a new world upon the ruins of what is always falling into decay."[17] If "ruins" expressed the discontent of the earlier era, "build a new world" was the vocational call Merton now held up to Catholics.

During the 1960s, Merton gave more attention to the new enthusiasm in the Church for interreligious dialogue. In the January 1961 issue of *Jubilee*, Merton wrote an article on "Classic Chinese Thought," in which he described Confucianism and Daoism as deeply ethical, religious thought and argued that Catholic colleges in the US should have courses in these traditions (still seen by many Catholics as little more than superstition). In 1966, he wrote of his dialogue with the Zen monk D. T. Suzuki. He had now moved well beyond his monastery's walls, newly attuned to the enchantment of faiths far outside the Catholic heritage.

In late 1968, Merton's journey beyond Trappist walls took him to Bangkok, Thailand, to participate in an international conference on world religions. During the conference, he touched an exposed electrical cord in his guest room and was electrocuted. His dramatic journey from the monastery to the world came to its completion. After his death, Merton's many written works would continue this expansion of the Catholic imagination in the direction of a more capacious and optimistic engagement with the world.

Dorothy Day: "All my life I have been haunted by God"

Dorothy Day, another failed novelist, was a Catholic author who had come of age in the 1920s and '30s. Like Merton, her essays and social initiatives in the 1950s signaled the emergence of a more optimistic and engaged spirituality that would foreshadow the seismic changes awaiting Catholics in the next decade and the Second Vatican Council.

Day's life reads like a catalogue of the first half of the century: she was a child in Oakland when the 1906 earthquake struck San Francisco; she celebrated with other socialists at Madison Square Garden in New York at the time of the Russian revolution

(1917); she founded the Catholic Worker Movement in the early 1930s in the teeth of the Depression; and she lobbied as a pacifist during World War II and the Korean War.

Day, like Merton, was a convert, becoming a Catholic in 1926, shortly after the birth of her daughter, Tamar Teresa. In her memoir, *The Long Loneliness*, Day recalls a passage in Dostoyevsky's *The Possessed* that seemed to describe her: "'All my life I have been haunted by God.'"[18] She writes of her early life when she first became conscious of the "idea of God as a tremendous Force, a frightening impersonal God, a Voice, a Hand stretched out to seize me, His child, and not in love."[19] This vision of "a frightening impersonal God" seizing her but "not in love" reiterates the Catholic God that we have seen in Waugh and Greene. In this same period, she first heard stories of the saints and became filled with "a lofty enthusiasm." Excited by this religious energy, she and her young friends "began to practice being saints."[20]

While still a teenager in Chicago, Day began reading accounts of the plight of the poor and came to suspect that her life must be involved in improving the lot of the disadvantaged. Day writes, "I wanted life and I wanted the abundant life. I wanted it for others too . . . and I did not have the slightest idea how to find it."[21] Day now began to dedicate her life to the search for life in abundance. And this longing was more than a personal or private piety. Her flourishing would have to include others as well. This focus on a life of abundance that was to be justly shared signaled a social activism and more engaged spirituality just arising in Catholic life at that time.

Part Two of Day's memoir is entitled "Man is Meant for Happiness," and in it, she recalls her own years of joy and delight in her ongoing relationship with Forster Batterham and the birth of her daughter, Tamar Teresa. Despite Day's reputation for living in austere conditions, this section of her memoir is dedicated to happiness. "I was happy, but my very happiness made me know that there was a greater happiness to be obtained from life than any I had ever known. I began to think, to weigh things, and it was at this time that I began consciously to pray."[22]

She mused on the reasons for this happiness. "I am praying because I am happy, not because I am unhappy. I did not turn to God in unhappiness, in grief, in despair—to get consolation, to get something from Him."[23] Day, unlike those in the Catholic tradition who seemed to oppose human love to divine love, was convinced that her love for Forster Batterham was the pathway to love of God. "I have always felt that it was life with him that brought me natural happiness, that brought me to God."[24] She writes, "I could not see that love between man and woman was incompatible with love of God."[25]

Something new was afoot in this vision of the sensual as portal to the spiritual. Or rather, something ancient was now being recovered in the Catholic imagination. "Because I was grateful for love, I was grateful for life, and living with Forster made me appreciate it and even reverence it still more. He had introduced me to so much that was beautiful and good that I felt I owed him too this renewed interest in the things of the spirit."[26]

Dorothy Day had great affection for a number of French Catholic authors who were expanding the range of the Catholic imagination. She appreciated Jacques Maritain's vision of a Christian humanism. When Maritain left the United States to take up his new position as France's ambassador to the Vatican (bringing several of Dorothy's essays from the Catholic Worker to give Pope Pius XII), she gave him a pair of socks that she had knitted for him. In an essay near the end of her life (May 1974), she invoked Teilhard de Chardin's eschatological vision: "Someday, after mastering the winds, the waves, the tides and gravity, we shall harness for God the energies of love, and then for the second time in the history of the world, man will discover fire."[27]

Dorothy Day's perspective on sainthood catches an important shift in the Catholic imagination. She was a great admirer of St. Thérèse of Lisieux, who died the year Day was born, 1897. Thérèse died at age twenty-four, living a virgin's cloistered life in a monastery in France. Dorothy Day would live out her eighty-three years exhaustingly engaged in social movements. Instead of a nun's solitude, Day had been involved in a number of sexual liaisons, had an abortion, and later gave birth to one daughter, Tamar Teresa.

Day rejected any suggestion of herself as a saint. "Don't call me a saint. I don't want to be dismissed that easily."[28] She then affirmed that we are all called to become saints; "there is some saint in all of us." While utterly devoted to St. Thérèse, Day argued for a new model of saintliness: "Where are the saints to try to change the social order?" [29] The ideal of sainthood, to which her own life witnessed, was of the messy, socially engaged variety.

Thomas Merton—now the maturing monk, not the young Trappist—and Dorothy Day were heralds of a Catholic imagination that was just taking shape in the 1950s. The continued influence of Merton and Day through the 1960s and beyond complemented the witness of French Catholic authors, especially Jacques Maritain with his endorsement of a Catholic humanism and Pierre Teilhard de Chardin with his witness to the enchantment of a cosmic spirituality.

Meanwhile, traces of an earlier Catholic imagination—one more focused on the disenchantment that continued to hem in Catholics—remained in evidence in the short stories of Flannery O'Connor and the novels of Walker Percy. We turn to these in the next two chapters.

[1] Flannery O'Connor, *Mystery and Manners*, 144. In the heading for this chapter, O'Connor comments on the state of the Catholic Church in the US in *A Habit of Being*, 308.

[2] Mary Gordon, *Final Payments*, 11.

[3] Brad Gooch, *Flannery: A Life of Flannery O'Connor*, 275.

[4] Evelyn Waugh's remark on "the divine purpose" appeared on the back jacket of the original edition of *Brideshead Revisited*.

[5] Gordon, 4.

[6] Gordon, 40–41.

[7] Paul Elie, *The Life You Save May Be Your Own: An American Pilgrimage*, 22.

[8] Thomas Merton, *The Seven Storey Mountain*, 383.

[9] Merton, 3.

[10] Merton, 73.

[11] Merton, 57.

[12] Merton, 409.

[13] Merton, 409.

[14] Merton, 417.

[15] Waugh, *Brideshead Revisited*, 31.

[16] Merton, *The Seven Storey Mountain*, 410.

[17] Merton, "The Second Coming," *Jubilee*, April 1956, 9.

[18] Day, *Selected Writings*, 9.

[19] Day, *The Long Loneliness*, 21.

[20] Day, 25.

[21] Day, 39.

[22] Day, 116.

[23] Day, 132.

[24] Day, 134.

[25] Day, 135.

[26] Day.

[27] Day, *Selected Writings*, 353, quoting Teilhard de Chardin's *Divine Milieu*.

[28] Day, xi.

[29] Day, *The Long Loneliness*, 45.

Chapter Six
Christians as *Necessary Misfits*

❦

Writers *"must often tell 'perverse' stories to 'shock' a morally blind world."*

—Brad Gooch, *Flannery: A Life of Flannery O'Connor*

Flannery O'Connor was a self-confessed outlier in the worlds she inhabited: a Catholic woman growing up in the Protestant South; a single person with neither husband nor children; plagued by chronic illness and often forced to use crutches. She relished the role of the disabled and turned it into a major theme in her short stories, populating them with the scarred and disfigured. *Misfit* was a category of being that O'Connor inhabited and turned to her own creative purposes. After hearing that Thomas Merton saw himself as a fourteenth-century Catholic, she went one better and insisted that she was a thirteenth-century Catholic. In the following stories, we will trace the links that connect outlier, misfit, and grotesque.

The Role of the Grotesque

O'Connor defended the grotesque as a style indigenous to the South, where it was celebrated by writers like William Faulkner and Carson McCullers. For O'Connor, the function of the grotesque was to reveal the brokenness of humans who are busy trying to disguise this feature. In an interview in *Jubilee* magazine in June 1963, O'Connor was asked why she so emphasized the grotesque; her straightforward answer: "We're all grotesque."[1] When readers complained that such oddballs and freaks did not exist, she would produce articles from rural Georgia newspapers of felons and follies that outdid her fictional characters. And O'Connor admitted that peopling her short stories with such characters was a literary strategy she found necessary. She used distortions and exaggerations to grab the attention of readers and convince them that something important was going on. Her conviction: "This is not the kind of distortion that destroys; it is the kind that reveals, or should reveal."[2] Literary critic Gregory Wolfe defended her penchant for misfits. "The grotesque in her fiction is not an unhealthy obsession with deformity but a metaphor for what we make of ourselves, the distortion that takes place when creatures attempt to think of themselves as gods, as creators of their own world."[3] Her biographer, Brad Gooch, adds, "O'Connor insisted that her own use of the grotesque was meant to convey a shocking Christian vision of original sin."[4]

In "A Good Man is Hard to Find," a family sets out on a trip. At a stop along the way, the restaurant proprietor laments, "A good man is hard to find. Everything is getting terrible. I remember the day you could go off and leave your screen door unlatched. Not no more."[5]

Shortly after resuming their travel, the driver loses control of the car and the family end up in a ditch. No one is seriously injured, and as the family sits pondering what to do next, they are happened upon by three escapees from a nearby federal prison. Their leader calls himself *The Misfit*. He explains his peculiar name: "I can't make all what I done wrong fit what all I gone through in punishment." As he and his two accomplices set about taking family members into a nearby woods and killing them, the grandmother prays aloud to Jesus. The Misfit responds, "Jesus thrown everything off balance. It was the same case with Him as with me except he hadn't committed any crime."[6] The last words between the grandmother and the Misfit lead the man to regret that he did not live in Jesus' time; if he had, he might not have gone down this psychopathic route. He then "shot her three times through the chest."[7]

O'Connor, in a letter in April 1960, tries to explain the spiritual dynamic at play here: "The Misfit is touched by the Grace that comes through the old lady when she recognizes him as her child, as she has been touched by the Grace that comes through him in his particular suffering."[8] After the Misfit kills the woman, O'Connor suggests that "the Grace has worked in him and he pronounces his judgment: she would have been a good woman if *he* had been there every moment of her life."[9] O'Connor was well aware that this transaction of grace was not evident to many readers.

In "The Life You Save May Be Your Own," a wandering tramp with a half-amputated arm arrives at a farmhouse inhabited by a woman and her daughter. On the first page we learn that the tramp's name is Mr. Shiftlet (not quite shiftless), and that the daughter is both nearsighted and mute. The tramp and the woman size each other up, agreeing that "the world is almost rotten."[10]

The woman and the tramp then commence bargaining about the man marrying the daughter, who the mother affirms is "fifteen, sixteen," though she is, in fact, thirty. The woman assures the tramp that her daughter, who is mute, is an ideal wife: "One that can't talk," she continued, "can't sass you back or use foul language."[11] The tramp agrees to marry the girl and inveigles seventeen dollars and fifty cents from the woman to pay for a honeymoon trip with the daughter in the aged car that he has recently rebuilt. He and the young woman leave on their "honeymoon," passing a sign alongside the road that warns, "Drive carefully. The life you save may be your own." When they stop at a café, the girl falls asleep at the counter; the tramp orders a meal for her and then abandons her as he continues on his way. Clouds gather in the distance as the tramp again muses on the rottenness of the world.

In "A Temple of the Holy Ghost," two teenage girls, staying at a friend's house for the weekend, are forever laughing and giggling. They call each other *Temple One* and *Temple Two* because the nun at their convent school had told them that they were to resist any sexual advances of boys since they were temples of the Holy Ghost.

The two girls, returning from a carnival they had visited that evening, tell a younger girl living at the house where they are staying about the freak they had seen in a sideshow. The freak had lifted her skirts, revealing that she was both man and woman. This person then warned the crowd, "God made me thisaway and if you laugh he may strike you the same way." The freak then insists, "This is the way He wanted me to be and I ain't disputing His way. I'm showing you because I got to make the best of it."[12]

The younger girl falls asleep thinking about all this. Then the next day, she and her mother arrange to have the two visiting girls returned to their convent school. When they arrive, the Catholic liturgy of Benediction is taking place. The girl's observance of this ceremony, with the elaborate monstrance containing the Host and the accompanying incense, is mixed in with her continued musing about the appearance of the freak and thoughts about everyone being a temple of the Holy Ghost. The short story concludes with an O'Connoresque sunset: "The sun was a huge red ball like an elevated Host drenched in blood and when it sank out of sight, it left a line in the sky like a red clay road hanging over the trees."[13] The author explained in a letter that this shocking image of an "elevated Host" in the sky was meant to echo the raised Host in the ritual of Benediction.

In a late prize-winning story, *Greenleaf*, O'Connor pits a bull against a woman with fatal results. The story begins with the woman aware that the bull is munching the bushes beneath her bedroom window "like some patient god come down to woo her."[14] The bull has managed to become entangled with a "hedge-wreath," which then slips down to the base of his horns and "looked like a menacing prickly crown."[15]

The woman is upset by the bull being loose once again on her property. Her efforts to get the tenant farmer, Mr. Greenleaf, or his two worthless sons to remove the bull fail. Finally she drives the tenant farmer with his shotgun into the field to find and destroy the animal.

Suddenly the beast charges her and impales her with his horns. "And the bull had buried his head in her lap, like a wild, tormented lover, before her expression had changed. One of his horns sank until it pierced her heart and the other curved around her side and held her in an unbreakable grip." When Mr. Greenleaf shoots the bull, "she did not hear the shots but she felt the quake in the huge body as it sank, pulling her forward on its head, so that she seemed, when Mr. Greenleaf reached her, to be bent over whispering some last discovery into the animal's ear."[16]

In 1952, O'Connor published her novel, *Wise Blood*. The title refers to a Southern saying concerning a native instinct that is received as a gift. The story follows the troubled life of Hazel "Haze" Motes, a twenty-two-year-old man who was a veteran of an unspecified war and a preacher of the Church of Truth Without Christ. The Church—a "religious" organization of Haze's own creation—serves to further his bitter, passion-fueled, and often spiteful words against anyone or anything representing a belief in God, an afterlife, judgment, sin, or evil.

O'Connor described the book as "a comic novel about a Christian *malgré lui,* and as such, very serious, for all comic novels that are any good must be about matters of life and death."[17] She sees the main character's integrity lies in his effort to shrug off Christian faith and, paradoxically, his inability to do so.

O'Connor's biographer describes Hazel Motes as "a more extreme character, a high-contrast and highly contrary prophet" who is further described as "going backwards to Bethlehem." Gooch adds, "He's the template for a number of memorable O'Connor creations who decide to operate their souls in reverse."[18] This evidently refers to O'Connor's preference for characters who are not only misfits but miscreants who then "operate their souls in reverse" by way of some kind of conversion.

As the novel nears its end, Haze is suddenly moved to a kind of conversion; he returns to his boardinghouse room and blinds himself with lime. In a letter of November 10, 1955, O'Connor acknowledges that many readers failed to make sense of this sudden self-destructive act. "The failure of the novel seems to be that he is not believable enough as a human being to make his blinding himself believable for the reasons that he did it."[19]

Motes is next seen wearing a penitential chain around his waist and placing stones in his shoes—signs of his sudden and extreme penitence. There are few clues in the story of what triggers this "conversion." In another letter, O'Connor attempts to explain the novel's conclusion. She describes Motes as "an admirable nihilist" whose "nihilism leads him back to the fact of his Redemption."[20] She acknowledges that "not too many are willing to see this."[21] What is more obvious is that O'Connor's Hazel Mote is an extreme version of a failed atheist in the tradition of Charles Ryder in *Brideshead Revisited* and Maurice Bendrix in *The End of the Affair.*

Reimagining the Communion of Saints

In the short story "Revelation," O'Connor presents a dazzling interpretation of the Catholic belief in the Communion of Saints. This core element in the Catholic imaginary envisions a transgenerational pilgrimage of believers—saints and sinners; the living and dead—moving in unison toward a final gathering in God. Theologian Elizabeth Johnson states: "The symbol signifies the relationship flowing among an intergenerational company of persons profoundly touched by the sacred, sharing in the cosmic community of life which is also sacred."[22]

In O'Connor's story, a woman looks up at the sky and seems to undergo a kind of revelation. "A visionary light settled in her eyes," and she seemed to see "a vast horde of souls [that] were rumbling toward heaven." In her typical fashion, O'Connor describes "whole companies of white-trash clean for the first time in their lives and bands of black negroes in white robes." Behind them came "battalions of freaks and lunatics shouting and clapping and leaping like frogs." And she noticed, "bringing up the end of the procession was a tribe of people whom she recognized at once as those who, like herself and Claude had always had a little of everything and the God-given wit to use it." This last group—her kind—were moving with great dignity and the only ones singing on key. "Yet she could see by their crooked and altered faces that even their virtues were being burned away." After the vision faded it seemed she could still hear "the voices of the souls climbing upward into the starry field and shouting hallelujah."[23]

In this tour de force, O'Connor reimagines the Communion of Saints in her own distinctive style: the entire retinue in her own imagination—the disfigured, the misfits, even the freaks—come together in a single enchanting procession. And her vision of "a vast horde of souls echoes the passage in the Letter to the Hebrews, "so great a cloud of witnesses" (12:1).

Testifying to Grace

O'Connor saw her vocation as testifying to the workings of grace in a world broken by original sin. In her letters, she repeatedly remarked about the wretchedness of the surrounding culture. "If you live today, you breathe in nihilism."[24] Her fictional characters repeatedly remark that "the world is almost rotten" and "everything is getting terrible." In such a climate, spiritual enchantment will arrive in brief epiphanies within environments blighted by broken and scarred souls.

She defined the special challenge of the Catholic novelist: "The fiction writer presents mystery through manners, grace through nature, but when he finishes there always has to be left over that sense of Mystery which cannot be accounted for by a human formula."[25]

In another letter, she further describes her notion of grace: "Grace, in the Catholic way of thinking, can and does use as its medium the imperfect, purely human, and even hypocritical."[26] For O'Connor, Grace (always capitalized in her letters) is refracted predominantly through the brokenness in humans. In an essay in *Mystery and Manners*, O'Connor describes the challenge of writing of grace: "Today's reader, if he believes in grace at all, sees it as something that can be separated from nature and served to him raw as Instant Uplift."[27]

Describing her own work in an essay in *Mystery and Manners*, she argues that "there is a moment in every great story in which the presence of grace can be felt as it waits to be accepted or rejected, even though the reader may not recognize this moment."[28] Her formula for the appearance of grace: "What is needed is an action that is totally unexpected, yet totally believable, and I have found that, for me, that is always an action which indicates that grace has been offered."[29]

In a letter of March 10, 1956, she returns to the challenge of describing grace. "Fiction is the concrete expression of mystery—mystery that is lived . . . it is almost impossible to write about supernatural Grace in fiction. We almost have to approach it negatively."[30] In another letter written that year, she judges that "it may be a matter of recognizing the Holy Ghost in fiction by the way He chooses to conceal himself."[31]

Catholics as *Necessary Misfits*

O'Connor, the self-confessed outlier, found her spirituality in the New Testament parables of being in the world but not of it. In John's gospel, Jesus warned his followers that "you do not belong to the world, but I have chosen you out of the world" (John 15:19). To follow Christ is to find oneself at odds with the surrounding culture, especially if, as O'Connor insisted, it promotes a climate of nihilism. Perhaps the Catholic faith demands that believers become necessary misfits.

Evelyn Waugh celebrated the eccentricities of the Catholic Marchmain family. A character in the novel observes how Catholics were outsiders in Anglican England: "Beware the Anglo-Catholics—they're all Sodomites with unpleasant accents."[32] For the convert Waugh, Catholics, with their allegiance to a foreign leader, the Pope, their prayers uttered in a foreign language, Latin, and their exotic pieties, were social misfits. But they were necessary misfits; this was an important part of their vocation.

James Joyce made himself an outsider: rejecting his Irish heritage, his stories return again and again to find their location in Ireland, especially Dublin. And denouncing his inherited Catholic faith, he drafts its symbols as a kind of second language.

Thomas Merton became an outlier by entering the monastery. As a celibate individual, withdrawn from the world, he cut a somewhat glamorous figure as a creative, even holy misfit. Dorothy Day, founder of the Catholic Worker, dedicated her life to misfits of every kind—the poor and homeless, alcoholics and infirmed. She too, professing Gospel values of caring for the poor and opposing the war in Vietnam, made herself an outcast, but like Merton, a misfit of considerable charm.

As we have seen, cultural change in America in the 1950s—greater access to higher education for Catholics—and a growing confidence in a rapprochement between faith and culture rendered a bunker mentality and a religious identity as outsider less imperative. With Vatican II, a deep suspicion of "the world" began to subside, being replaced by an engagement in ordinary life and expressing one's faith in the social structures of the surrounding society. We will see how novelists Mary Gordon and Marilynne Robinson turn their attention away from this more insular mood and self-definition as outsider in favor of an engagement in "the rituals of the ordinary."[33]

Afterthoughts

O'Connor grew up Irish Catholic in the South, where Catholics were a minority, still at odds with the broader culture. Her first school, St. Vincent's, she remembered as "an enclave of parochialism of the sort she would later label the 'novena-rosary tradition.'"[34] She sojourned in the North for only five years in her early twenties. She first earned a graduate degree in writing at the University of Iowa, where her southern accent was a source of amusement.

At the University of Iowa, a teacher arranged an opportunity for her to spend time at the writers' colony Yaddo in Vermont. There she had her first taste of what a career in writing might look like. Through a budding friendship with the poet Robert Lowell, she met Robert Giroux (later of Farrar, Straus & Giroux), a like-minded Catholic who would edit and champion her short stories and novel.

In the many lectures she gave in the late 1950s and early 1960s, she stoutly defended her Southern culture, believing its "Christ-haunted" society was a fitting seed-bed for stories that might illumine the role of religious faith in a nation rapidly turning secular. She did not much like other southern women writers. She disliked the stories of Carson McCullers, who returned the sentiment. (McCullers had published *The Heart is a Lonely Hunter* at age twenty-three when O'Connor was fifteen and suspected that O'Connor was later borrowing from her own style of southern gothic.) Responding to the great success of Harper Lee's *To Kill a Mockingbird*, O'Connor remarked that it was a wonderful children's book.

In 1950, at age twenty-five and while still at Yaddo, she contracted lupus, which was at first misdiagnosed as rheumatoid arthritis. She returned home to her farm in Milledgeville, Georgia, where she lived the next four-teen years of her life with her mother and died in 1964 at age thirty-nine.

Having finished a draft of this book, we came across a letter O'Connor wrote in the last months of her life, when she seemed to endorse the scope of this book. She was responding to an invitation by a priest to lecture to his class about Catholic novelists. Her illness caused her to refuse the invitation; then she added: "You could tell them that anybody who wants to be introduced to Catholic fiction will have to start with the French— Mauriac and Bernanos . . . the English are Waugh and Greene." She adds that among American authors, she favors "Percy (our friend Walker)" and that "the most important non-fiction writer is Pere Pierre Teilhard de Chardin, S.J. who died in 1955 and has so far escaped the Index."[35] In another letter, written in 1957, she repeated her endorsement of these authors, adding that in comparison, "the Americans seem just to be produc-ing pamphlets for the back of the church."[36]

For some readers today, O'Connor's short stories sport too many maimed and ruined humans. To others, her stories resonate with religious convictions about the enduring fruits of original sin. Whatever the merits of her fiction, rewards were eventually forthcoming. Her *Complete Stories* was awarded the National Book Award for Fiction in 1972, and her collection of letters, *The Habit of Being*, received the National Book Critics Circle Special Award for 1979.

1   Flannery O'Connor, *Mystery and Manners*, 233.
2   Flannery O'Connor, *Mystery and Manners*, 162.
3   Gregory Wolfe, *Beauty Will Save the World*, 100.
4   Gooch, 289.
5   Flannery O'Connor, "A Good Man is Hard to Find," *The Complete Stories*, 122.
6   O'Connor, 131.
7   O'Connor, 132.
8   O'Connor, *The Habit of Being*, 389.
9   O'Connor, 189.
10 O'Connor, "The Life You Save May Be Your Own," *The Complete Stories*, 146.
11 O'Connor, 151.
12 O'Connor, "A Temple of the Holy Ghost," *The Complete Stories*, 245.
13 O'Connor, 248.
14 O'Connor, "Greenleaf," *The Complete Stories*, 311.
15 O'Connor, 312
16 O'Connor, 334.
17 O'Connor, *Mystery and Manners*, 114.
18 Gooch, 7.
19 O'Connor, *Mystery and Manners*, 116.
20 O'Connor, *The Habit of Being*, 70.
21 O'Connor.
22 Elizabeth Johnson, *Friends of God and Prophets: A Feminist Theological Reading of the Communion of Saints*, 2.
23 O'Connor, "Revelation," *The Complete Stories*, 491.
24 O'Connor, *The Habit of Being*, 97.
25 O'Connor, *Mystery and Manners*, 153.
26 O'Connor, *The Habit of Being*, 389.
27 O'Connor, *Mystery and Manners*, 165.
28 O'Connor, 118.
29 O'Connor.
30 O'Connor, *The Habit of Being*, 144.
31 O'Connor, 130.
32 Evelyn Waugh, *Brideshead Revisited*, 26.
33 Marilynne Robinson, *Housekeeping*, 16.
34 Gooch, 29.
35 *The Habit of Being*, 570.
36 *The Habit of Being*, 231.

Chapter Seven
The Disenchantment of
Everydayness

*"The search is what anyone would undertake if he were not
sunk in the everydayness of his own life."*

—Walker Percy, *The Moviegoer*

Walker Percy, in his 1961 novel, *The Moviegoer*, paints
a portrait of modern disenchantment in the metaphor
of everydayness. Binx Bolling is a twenty-nine-year-old
unmarried stockbroker in New Orleans. A veteran of
the Korean War, he suffers from a chronic depression
that is associated with his inability to find any sub-
stantial purpose in life—what he names the blight of
everydayness. His cousin Kate inquires of him, "How do
you make your way in the world?" Later his aunt asks
him, "What is it you want out of life, son?" These are
precisely the questions that haunt him; his inability to
discover an answer to these core questions leaves him
adrift in a miasma of chronic *everydayness.*

"Everydayness is the enemy. No search is possible. Perhaps there was a time when everydayness was not too
strong and one could break its grip by brute strength."
Binx reflects further, his thoughts now in parenthesis:
"(The everydayness is everywhere now, having begun
in the cities and seeking out the remotest nooks and cor-
ners of the countryside, even the swamps.)" This mood

of disenchantment leads, for Binx, to the affliction of malaise. "What is the malaise? you ask. The malaise is the pain of loss. The world is lost to you, the world and the people in it."[1] Percy suggests that this affliction is not simply Binx's; it is a mark of modern life.

This everydayness and the malaise it induces obstruct "the search"—those exceptional moments when a person might come alive and the quest for meaning and purpose seems possible. "The search is what anyone would undertake if he were not sunk in the everydayness of his own life."[2] Binx is aware that "to become aware of the possibility of the search is to be onto something. Not to be onto something is to be in despair." He is keenly aware that he has not "been onto something" for a long time.

He sums up his dreadful current condition: "For years now I have had no friends. I spend my entire time working, making money, going to movies and seeking the company of women."[3] Percy names here two strategies of distraction that Binx employs to hold off his despair. He goes regularly to the movies (hence, the title of the novel), finding that the cinematic lives in the theater provide some brief relief from life's boredom. Moviegoing functions as a faux enchantment that assuages, for the moment, the blight of his depression and despair. The other faux enchantment is his superficial flirtation with his serially hired secretaries (Marcia, Linda, Sharon). Nothing ever comes of these flirtations, but they do hold off for the moment the descent back into "malaise."

Binx has found that his depression lifts and the possibility of "the search" returns only in times of extremity, of crisis. The first experience of such a crisis was his being wounded in the Korean War. Awaking from a blast, he found himself alive and attuned to life in a way that he has since been unable to repeat. Later, a powerful Southern storm got his attention and he managed to clear away, for the length of the storm, the chronic sense of everydayness. "A storm breaks . . . gradually the malaise lets up." A minor car accident, while traveling with one of his secretaries in his MG, likewise yanked him out of his black mood for a brief, refreshing moment. His cousin Kate, who suffers from depression and probably a bipolar condition, has the same experience of time. "I am always at my best with doctors. They are charmed with me. I feel fine when I'm sick."[4]

War, storms, accidents, illness: these troubling events break into and upset, for the time being, the everydayness that is the blight on Binx's existence. Apart from these extreme moments, movies and brief affairs provide some relief from "everydayness." These events verify—Binx calls it "certification"—one's earthly existence and, for a brief period, a person can feel genuinely alive. These times-out-of-time afford an individual a sense of being "a person who is Somewhere and not Anywhere."[5] For the moment, a person feels present to his life, not lost in a mindless universe. Kate explains her attempted suicide in a similar fashion: "I didn't want to die—not at that moment. I only wanted to—break out, or off, off dead center—Listen. Isn't it true that the only happy men are wounded men?"[6]

In his second novel, Percy returns to this role of crisis, especially nature's storms, in lifting the malaise that habitually envelops his heroes. Walter Isaacson notes that "Will Barrett in *The Last Gentleman* found that a hurricane 'blew away the sad, noxious particles which befoul the sorrowful old Eastern sky and Midge no longer felt obliged to keep her face stiff.'"[7] After the storm, Midge became happy as she helped a man with a broken window. "Everything was yellow and still and charged with value."[8] Isaacson adds, "Percy's diagnosis was that when we are mired in the everydayness of ordinary life we are susceptible to what he called 'the malaise,' a free-floating despair associated with the feeling that you're not part of the world or connected to people in it."[9]

In *The Moviegoer*, Binx reflects that when he meets a Jewish person he is alerted again to the search; he senses he is somehow getting closer to discovering some meaning and purpose in life. He shares, at least, the same loss of enchantment that Jews experience. "We share the same exile . . . I accept my exile."[10] Disenchantment, for Percy and other Catholic authors of the twentieth century, is a form of exile: one is dislocated from the source of enchantment, and even from the ability to undertake the search.

Binx finds little solace or direction from his relatives. Uncle Jules is a man of the world: the only person Binx knows who lives contentedly in the everydayness of life. He is Catholic, but "it is hard to know why he takes the trouble."[11] He is so content in "the City of Man" that "the City of God" would seem to hold little attraction for him. An aunt confesses her own defeatist stoicism. One should simply do one's best, although "in this world goodness is destined to be defeated. But a man must go down fighting. That is the victory."[12]

The first two chapters of the novel end with ominous portraits of his cousin Kate's chronic depression. "In her long nightmare, this our old friendship now itself falls victim to the grisly transmogrification by which she unfailingly turns everything she touches to horror."[13] And, at the close of chapter two, Kate is suddenly mightily enthused about some insight that, after twenty-five years of trying to please others, has set her free. Binx muses grimly that he has seen this mood swing, with its great but brief revelations, before. These chapter endings serve to establish Kate's dire condition, setting up the conclusion of the novel when Binx, himself finally delivered of needing to please others, is able to exit his chronic malaise and marry Kate.

As the novel nears its conclusion, Binx is asked by his Uncle Jules to attend a stockbrokers' convention in Chicago. Kate impulsively decides to accompany him, and they begin a train ride to Chicago. On the way, these longtime friends attempt to make love, and the effort fails badly. This gives Percy the opportunity to provide some authorial comment. Beauty, we are told, is an illusion when we seek to find all life's meaning in this aspect of life. "Beauty, the quest of beauty alone, is a whoredom."[14] Binx had earlier tried this remedy, plunging himself into a quest for beauty in music, and it did not relieve the blight of everydayness. So it is with sexuality. As Binx and Kate attempt to have sex in the hope that the dalliance might deliver them of their malaise, this too must fail. "Flesh, poor flesh failed us. The burden was too great and the flesh poor flesh, neither hallowed by sacrament nor despised by spirit" was not up to it. "Flesh, poor flesh now at this moment

summoned all at once to be all and everything, end all
and be all, the last and only hope—quails and fails."[15]
For Percy, both beauty and sex, when we ask too much
of them, are no more than faux enchantments. (One
might just as well go to the movies.)

In Chicago, the couple visit Binx's wartime buddy
who had saved his life in Korea. Shortly after that,
the couple is called home by an angry phone call from
Binx's aunt. She had assumed, when Kate disappeared
without telling anyone she was going to Chicago with
Binx, that she might have again attempted suicide.
The aunt was both relieved and outraged to find that
Kate had gone off with Binx, with Binx not bothering
to inform her or others in the family. When Binx and
Kate return to New Orleans, the aunt unloads on him,
accusing him of irresponsible behavior. In her tirade she
emphasizes the family's class status and their heritage as
expectations for Binx to live up to. Percy may be sug-
gesting that is precisely this shroud of social expectation
that had enveloped Binx in his malaise. As he stands
before his aunt, weathering her indictment, her anger
seems to cleanse him of the everydayness of his life.
With this unexpected change, he found he was no longer burdened with his chronic search for meaning. "My
search has been abandoned; it is no match for my aunt,
her rightness and her despair."[16]

Shriven of the need to fit in, to please others, Binx
discovers that he is suddenly free. Now he is able to
see Kate with a clarity that approaches that of his wartime experience. "There I see her plain, see plain for the
first time since I lay wounded in a ditch and watched
an Oriental finch scratching around in the leaves."[17]

This deliverance allows Binx to commit himself to marry Kate in all her vulnerability. They are now able to emerge from the cloud of disenchantment that had haunted both of their lives.

Percy's editor at Knopf, Stanley Kauffmann, had doubts about the abruptness of this ending. He wondered, "What takes the agony out of living for Binx and Kate?" What accounted for this sudden change of heart in Binx? Kauffmann observed that "the effect is as if someone had suddenly switched on a lot of rosy lights." Skilled at describing the existential angst of his hero, Percy has trouble making believable the sudden transformation that forms the denouement of the novel. Indeed, as reviews came in for the publication, Percy was alarmed that some reviewers read the book as a story of despair. They had missed the sudden and not quite accountable uplift or enchantment that Percy thought he had injected into the closing pages.

Like Charles Ryder in *Brideshead Revisited* and Maurice Bendrix in *The End of the Affair*, Binx Bolling makes a show of rejecting religious belief; he struggles to adjust to a disenchanted life. But the effort cannot prevail. Like these other literary creations by Catholic authors in the first half of the twentieth century, Binx is a failed atheist.

The Dangers of Catholicizing

Walker Percy worried about the temptation of authors like himself to "Catholicize" their fiction. "It is almost impossible to Catholicize, pro or con, without falling on your face."[18] Flannery O'Connor, in her usual caustic fashion, concurred: "When the Catholic novelist closes his eyes and tries to see with the eyes of the Church, the result is another addition to that large body of pious trash for which we have for so long been famous."[19] She further indicts "the sorry religious novel" in which the author thinks the Church "has already done the seeing for him and that his business is to re-arrange this essential vision into satisfying patterns, getting himself as little dirty in the process as possible."[20]

For authors equipped with the second language of Christian faith, it is indeed tempting to dress their characters in the finery of Catholic practice. And this is a temptation not always resisted. Graham Greene has the failed Catholic Scobie, in *The Heart of the Matter*, carry around "a broken rosary." George Bernanos has his priest's stomach troubles reduce him to a (sacramental) diet of "bread and wine." Flannery O'Connor creates a character who raises his arms (one arm is, of course, partially amputated) until his figure appears on the horizon in the shape of a crucifix. The conclusion of her short story "Temple of the Holy Ghost" includes this garish image of a sunset: "The sun was a huge red ball like an elevated Host drenched in blood and when it sank out of sight, it left a line in the sky like a red clay road hanging over the trees."

During the decade of the 1950s, when Percy was producing early drafts of his *The Moviegoer* and Flannery O'Connor was crafting her short stories, a subgenre of Catholic fiction was enjoying some popularity. J. F. Powers produced a number of short story collections that focused almost exclusively on the Catholic parish. As in *The Presence of Grace* (1956), the central characters were reliably the pastor, the assistant priest, the housekeeper, and often a woman parishioner. There was no "Catholicizing" in these stories since they were only and always about parish and rectory matters.

Many Catholic authors were drawn to locate their stories within the infrastructure of the liturgical year—especially Ash Wednesday and Holy Week. These are times for special attention and potential transformations, and so become obvious vehicles for a plot's spiritual progress. Here questions of literary merit arise only when an author puts too much weight on these times to move the plot in a kind of *deus ex machina*. Percy and O'Connor's concern about "Catholicizing" was a worry about the temptation to provoke spiritual enchantment on the cheap.

The Catholic Imagination: Redeeming the Time

Percy, reader of Camus and Sartre, was a master at describing the malaise and disenchantment that he saw in midcentury America; he was, in fact, struggling to redeem the time. Like T. S. Eliot forty years earlier, Percy was trying to describe how the flow of time can be rescued from its pointlessness in a disenchanted world. The Catholic imagination has always included attention to time—how Christians are to spend their days in the light of eternity. St. Paul in his letter to the Christians in Ephesus urged that community to pay special attention to the rhythm of their days. "Be careful, then, how you live. . . . Redeem the time" (Ephesians 5:16 King James Version). Paul was not advocating multitasking. He was encouraging this first generation of Christians to avoid squandering their precious days in wasteful distractions.

Binx Bolling, the central character in *The Moviegoer*, has too much time on his hands; his days are weighted with an unrelieved monotony. He only comes alive in moments of emergency: wartime, storms, car accidents. Philosopher Roberto Unger, in his analysis of boredom, might be commenting on Percy's novel. "Boredom is . . . the weight of unused capacity, an intimation of the freedom from which the self has hidden." In boredom, we find nothing that invites our commitment or calls for any risk. Now our only excitement will be found in what Unger defines as diversion—"the search for novelty without peril."[21] Unger offers a precise measurement of Binx's earlier life: "The failed life is the life that alternates between the stagnation of routinized conduct and vision and the restless craving for momentary release."[22] For Binx, moviegoing provides this momentary but ultimately unsatisfying release.

Faithful to his Catholic and Southern roots, Percy situates the novel during Carnival time in New Orleans just before the beginning of Lent. In the weeks preceding Mardi Gras, various civic clubs (krewes) launch parades with flamboyant floats and people strut about in outrageous costumes. These days before Ash Wednesday are a kind of time-out-of-time: cavorting of every kind is the order of the week in this brief interval before the beginning of the more sober period of Lent. The Carnival and Mardi Gras serve for Percy as examples of another kind of faux enchantment that, for a brief period, offer "momentary release."

When Bing and Kate leave New Orleans for Chicago, they miss out on the celebrations of Mardi Gras. When they return, the party is over; it is already Ash

Wednesday; they notice people coming out of churches with smudges of ash on their foreheads. This sequence in the novel is not accidental. Percy is making a point about time: the faux enchantment of Mardi Gras is skipped over and genuine change (Binx committing himself to marriage with Kate) takes place in the different kind of time begun with Ash Wednesday. Lent begins, and Binx's new life starts up: the faux enchantments of moviegoing and brief affairs are set aside; in his commitment to Kate, time sheds it chronic *everydayness* and a better life begins.

The subtitle of Percy's second novel, *Love in the Ruins*, telegraphs his negative view of current conditions in the US and beyond: *The Adventures of a Bad Catholic at a Time near the End of the World.* In a recent essay in *Commonweal* magazine, Edward Dupuy argues that Percy's pessimism insists that this wretched age must perish before a new era can begin. The novelist's depiction of apocalyptic times "becomes an avenue of recovery." With the reforms of the Second Vatican Council, this pessimism lost much of its foothold in Catholic culture.

Literature and religion are both concerned with shaping the unstoppable flow of time to human purposes. Literary critic Gregory Wolfe describes his own efforts to redeem the time: "to explore the relationship between religion, art, and culture in order to discover how the imagination might 'redeem the time.'"[23] For Wolfe, the imagination—its vitality and reach—is the clue to an appreciation of enchantment and the path toward a redeeming of time. Christian Wiman, in *My Bright Abyss*, adds this note: "Faith cannot save you from the claims of reason, except insofar as it preserves and protects *that wonderful, terrible time* when reason, if only for a moment, lost its claim on you."[24] Such moments— times of grace that are both "wonderful and terrible"— are invitations to enchantment.

*   *   *   *   *   *   *

Running through the stories of Flannery O'Connor and Walker Percy is a spirituality of disenchantment. Both experienced themselves as outsiders and regularly disparaged the American culture that surrounded and threatened their faith. During the 1950s, a very different spirituality was stirring in this country. Catholics were just being introduced to the optimistic Christian humanism of Jacques Maritain and the cosmic evolutionary hopes of Teilhard de Chardin. We turn to this spiritual perspective in the next chapter.

Afterthoughts

Walker Percy contracted tuberculosis just as he was finishing his medical studies in the 1940s. He had already lost both parents and a grandfather to suicide. Once recovered, he decided not to return to the medical profession but to attempt to become a writer. With this decision he plunged into reading existentialist authors. His portrayal of boredom in *The Moviegoer* owes much to Camus and Sartre, with no little help from Kierkegaard.

Percy married in 1946, and the couple adopted a daughter and then had a second daughter. The couple became Catholics in 1947 when Percy was thirty-one years old. Throughout the 1950s, he worked on several novels and published essays on modernity and the search for meaning in various journals such as *Thought* and *Commonweal*. His first novel, *The Moviegoer*, was published in 1961 and received The National Book Award.

[1] Walker Percy, *The Moviegoer*, 120.

[2] Percy, 13.

[3] Percy, 31.

[4] Percy, 81.

[5] Percy, 63.

[6] Percy, 181.

[7] Walter Isaacson, "Walker Percy's Theory of Hurricanes," *The New York Times Sunday Book Review*.

[8] Isaacson.

[9] Isaacson.

[10] Percy, *The Moviegoer*, 89.

[11] Percy, 31.

[12] Percy, 54.

[13] Percy, 63.

[14] Percy, 196.

[15] Percy, 200.

[16] Percy, 228.

[17] Percy, 206.

[18] Patrick Samway, *Walker Percy: A Life*, 205.

[19] Flannery O'Connor, *Mystery and Manners*, 180.

[20] O'Connor, 170.

[21] Roberto Unger, *Passion: An Essay on Personality*, 112.

[22] Unger.

[23] Wolfe, 2.

[24] Christian Wiman, *My Bright Abyss*, 7.

Chapter Eight
Catholic Enchantment:
French Accents, Part Two

"What the world needs is a new humanism, a 'theocentric' or integral humanism which would consider man in all his natural grandeur and weakness, in the entirety of his wounded being inhabited by God, in the full reality of nature, sin and sainthood."

—Jacques Maritain

During the 1950s, the writings of two French Catholics were gaining attention in the United States. The Catholic philosopher Jacques Maritain was teaching at Princeton University as the decade began. The scientist-theologian Pierre Teilhard de Chardin's ideas on a spirituality of evolution—a kind of cosmic imagination—were just beginning to enchant American Catholics.

If Maritain turned the attention of American Catholics toward an engagement with others in society, Teilhard would shift their attention to the entire universe. Maritain's vision of a Christian humanism was complemented by Teilhard's mystical view of an enchanted cosmos. Both of these authors promoted a more optimistic Catholic imagination and an enchanted vision of Christian life in the modern world.

Jacques Maritain: A Christian Humanism

Jacques Maritain, born the same year as James Joyce (1882), was to American Catholics a novel figure: former French ambassador to the Vatican, he was a public intellectual comfortable with and respected by non-Catholic scholars. A convert to Catholicism, Maritain had lectured at various universities in Canada and the US, and in 1948 took a position at Princeton University. He was especially pleased with this appointment: "In no European university would I have found the spirit of liberty and congeniality I found at Princeton in teaching moral philosophy in the light of Thomas Aquinas." A Catholic teaching at a non-Catholic university was a novelty at midcentury, and a sign of things to come. (Another Catholic, the British-born Christopher Dawson, would at the end of the 1950s be named the first occupant of a chair in Catholic Studies at Harvard University Divinity School.)

Readers of *Jubilee* magazine in November 1957 caught a glimpse of Maritain's vision of "The Christian and History." Maritain, then seventy-five years old, reflected on the long reach of history and the movement toward the kingdom of God. This notion, so familiar today, appeared as a novel image to many readers. Maritain gave an energizing shape to this theological image: "The work of the Christian is to maintain and augment in the world the internal tension and movement of slow deliverance which are due to the invisible potencies of truth and justice and love."[1]

Thomas Merton and Flannery O'Connor were especially intrigued by Maritain's essays about the links between art and Christian virtue. No Catholic had previously spoken of art—for these authors, the art of writing—as a virtue. These American authors were also delighted with Maritain's description of the artist's vocation. The power of art "frees from every human care, it establishes . . . artist or artisan, in a world apart, cloistered, defined and absolute, in which to devote all the strength and intelligence of his manhood to the service of the thing which he is making."[2] And they were intrigued by Maritain's description of the virtue of prudence as it seemed to apply to their own vocation as Catholic authors: "Prudence discerns and applies the means of attaining our moral ends, which are themselves subordinate to the ultimate end of all human life—that is to say, God." In his reverie of art in the medieval Christian world, Maritain introduced the notion of enchantment: "Beauty [was something that] faith kept enchanted and led after it obedient, with a gossamer thread for leash."[3]

Maritain's greatest contribution to American Catholic life may have been his vision of Christian humanism. This concept, unfamiliar to American Catholics at midcentury who still inhabited a rather insular and defensive faith, implied a comfort with and optimism about the culture in which they found themselves. If they knew anything about humanism, they likely associated it with atheists who insisted that humans themselves are our sole concern. The Vatican II text on the Church in the modern world spoke to a new openness to all humans and their deepest aspirations: "Nothing that is genuinely human fails to find an echo in their [Christian] hearts."[4] Maritain's essays would help Catholics reclaim this optimism about God's presence within every culture.

"What the world needs is a new humanism, a 'theo-centric' or integral humanism which would consider man in all his natural grandeur and weakness, in the entirety of his wounded being inhabited by God, in the full reality of nature, sin and sainthood."[5] Maritain defined what a Christian humanism would look like. "Let us say that humanism . . . essentially tends to render man more truly human and to make his original greatness manifest by causing him to participate in all that can enrich him in nature and in history."[6] Humanism "at once demands that man make use of all the potentialities he holds within him, his creative powers and the life of the reason, and labour to make the powers of the physical world the instruments of his freedom."[7]

Humanism, for Maritain, meant an affirmation of all that is good in this world, with the acknowledgment that humans aspire to something else and something more. "The idea we form of humanism will have wholly different implications according to whether we hold that there is in the nature of man something which breathes an air outside of time and a personality whose profoundest needs surpass the order of the universe."[8]

A Devout Humanism

Maritain set out to show that the impulses of humanism have their roots in Christian history itself; humanism was not a child of secular modernity. "Western humanism springs from religious and 'transcendental' sources, without which it would be incomprehensible even to itself."[9] Maritain reminded Catholics that in the Middle Ages, humans pictured themselves as part of a rich, complex reality governed by God. Scholars today have amplified Maritain's intuitive sense of "a devout humanism." Philosopher of religion Louis Dupré locates the taproot of this optimism near the end of the eleventh century "when a fresh awareness of the Incarnation as a cosmically transforming event" led, in art (Cimabue's crucifixes of the suffering Jesus), spirituality (Francis of Assisi's affection for nature), and theology (Bernard of Clairvaux on the *Song of Songs*) to a more optimistic embrace of nature as suffused with God's presence. "Christians once again came to trust the impulses of nature."[10]

And in the fifteenth century, Ignatius of Loyola furthered this new optimistic humanism with his conviction about "finding God in all things." As Dupré has observed, Ignatius was convinced that individuals, trained in an ascetical method of discernment, could develop "the capacity to perceive the delicate, highly personal touches of grace" in their lives and discern the "spirits"—good or bad—influencing these movements of their hearts.[11]

Catholic humanism—for Maritain at midcentury and many Catholic scholars today—aspires to a "rehabilitation of the creature in God."[12] The self-consciousness that is a central part of modern culture need not be a disenchanted consciousness of humans in isolation, with freedom but no greater purpose. It can be a consciousness of humans with all their aspirations for more life, for a more generous and grateful existence.

The marriage of humanism and Christian faith continues to animate many today. Gregory Wolfe, in his

Beauty Will Save the World, recalls the judgment of the scholar of comparative literature Virgil Nemoianu: "Christian humanism is nothing but reclaiming the basic inheritance of the world as it is: the natural and organic connection between the works of culture and the religious roots and vistas of the human being."[13]

Teilhard de Chardin's Cosmic Imagination

"This is a scientific age and Teilhard's direction is to face it toward Christ."

—Flannery O'Connor in a letter dated April 9, 1960

Pierre Teilhard de Chardin was a French Jesuit paleontologist who participated in excavations in China in the 1920s that led to the discovery of *Peking Man*. While pursuing his scientific explorations into the origins of humankind, he began to envision a cosmic evolution that would culminate in a final unity of all reality in God. During the 1950s, Teilhard's mystical writings were just beginning to be noticed by American Catholics. As O'Connor read more of Teilhard's work, she wrote that "I think myself he was a great mystic."[14] And, she confessed in a letter written the next year, "I'm much taken, though, with père Teilhard . . . he was alive to everything there is to be alive to and in the right way."[15]

The Enchantment of Evolution

American Catholics at midcentury were, like most other Christians, unsure about the scope of human evolution.

A radical reworking of the age the cosmos seemed to put the biblical accounts of creation into doubt. How could the creation of Adam and Eve be squared with billions of years of evolution—with humans appearing only very recently?

To Teilhard, the entire universe, from its inception, has been animated by the guiding presence of God's Spirit. This dynamic presence moves the universe through an evolution that continues to gather up matter into a spiritual consciousness, pointing to a final unification of all things in Christ. Creation is not a once-and-for-all event; it is the very unfolding or evolution of history. In his two most important books, *The Phenomenon of Man* and *The Divine Milieu* (both published only after his death in 1955), Teilhard sketched out his evolutionary vision. Matter evolves first into what he names the geosphere, and then into the living matter he calls the biosphere. Life in turn evolves into human consciousness, the noosphere, and finally into the Omega Point which is the cosmic Christ. In this vision, spiritual development is moved by the same laws as those that trigger material development.

In this vision, evolution is not a mindless expansion of matter, but the very process where the history of salvation is taking place. In this realization, humans discover that they are evolution that has become conscious of itself. It would take some decades for this sense of cosmic enchantment to find its way into the awareness of American Catholics.

American Catholics were introduced to Teilhard and his evolutionary view of *The Phenomenon of Man* in the September 1959 issue of *Jubilee*.[16] O'Connor entitled her collection of short stories *Everything That Rises Must Converge*—a phrase from Teilhard's writings.

Teilhard's mystic vision of God's animating presence in the whole universe both turned Catholics' attention outward but also encouraged a recognition of salvation as a collective adventure. He insisted that Christian life is not a matter of individual devotion or a private piety, but a collaborative and collective ascent of all humanity toward a final unity in God. "No evolutionary future awaits anyone except in association with everyone else." This communal orientation in Teilhard's spirituality was matched by the ongoing liturgical reform during the 1960s that was encouraging American Catholics to turn from an individualistic piety toward a shared celebration of the sacraments.

Teilhard's theology grew out of his reading of the New Testament. He sought to apply his vision of evolution to Paul's belief that "in Christ, God was reconciling the world with Godself" (2 Corinthians 5:19; our translation). For Teilhard, Paul's image of "the body of Christ" was more than a mystic metaphor for the Church; it represented a cosmic imagination. The cosmic Christ, for Teilhard, "is the whole inner energy of the universe and the goal to which all of the universe is moving."[17]

In the Catholic Church today, Teilhard's imaginative vision of evolution seems less radical. In recent decades, historians have recovered the works of such theologians of the Eastern Church as Gregory of Nyssa. Gregory, a contemporary of St. Augustine, described a vision in which all persons would be gathered up, at the end time, into God. Theologians in the Eastern Church spoke of this ultimate unfolding of human life as "a divinization"—a spiritual evolution that was either forgotten or denied by theologians in the Western Church.

Not surprisingly, Teilhard's mystical ruminations on the *divine milieu* met with severe resistance during his lifetime. Such an optimistic vision seemed to neglect the force of original sin and to assume that all persons would ultimately be brought together in a final unity in Christ. The Catholic imaginary that dominated the first half of the century was deeply influenced by St. Augustine's pessimism that predicted a dark outcome for the mass of humanity, with only the elect being saved by God's inscrutable predestination.

Teilhard was repeatedly instructed not to teach or publish any of his writing. Even two years after his death, the Holy Office in the Vatican forbade the inclusion of any of his writing in church libraries or bookshops. When he died on Easter Sunday in 1955 at age seventy-three, none of his writings had been published. In his last years he had trusted his manuscripts to friends who saw that his bold ideas might be published after his death. Flannery O'Connor commented on this fellow writer: if Teilhard was faithful to Jesuit obedience in his life, "he must have figured that in death he would be a citizen of some other sphere and that the fate of his books with the Church would rest with the Lord."[18] He was not to see the vindication of his works that would occur after the Second Vatican Council, but we might guess that, with his usual optimism, he had quietly foreseen this aspect of a cosmic evolution.

In the second half of the century, as the Catholic imagination became more expansive, making room for his enchanting vision of the *divine milieu*, many theologians and Church leaders (Popes John Paul II and Benedict XVI among them) made haste to endorse his creative and enchanting vision. Cardinal Christoph Schönborn wrote in 2007: "Hardly anyone else has tried to bring together the knowledge of Christ and the idea of evolution as the scientist (paleontologist) and theologian Fr. Pierre Teilhard de Chardin, S.J. has done." Schönborn added, "His fascinating vision . . . has represented a great hope that faith in Christ and a scientific approach to the world can be brought together."[19]

Afterthoughts

Jacques Maritain (1882–1973) met his future wife and intellectual partner, Raïssa Oumançoff, a Russian Jewish émigré, while they were studying at the Sorbonne. In 1901, in the midst of their shared disenchantment with life, they made a pact to commit suicide together if they could not discover some deeper meaning to life within a year. They had the good fortune of meeting, during this time, the Catholic poet Charles Péguy who encouraged them to attend the lectures of Henri Bergson at the *Collège de France*. Bergson's critique of scientism dissolved their intellectual despair. They married in 1904 and entered the Catholic Church two years later.

Maritain immersed himself in the study of Thomas Aquinas, and in 1933 he gave his first lectures in North America in Toronto at the Pontifical Institute of Mediaeval Studies. He also taught at Columbia University; at the Committee on Social Thought, University of Chicago; at the University of Notre Dame, and at Princeton University. From 1945 to 1948, he was the French ambassador to the Vatican. Many of his American papers are held by the University of Notre Dame, which established The Jacques Maritain Center in 1957.

Pierre Teilhard de Chardin (1881–1955) was ordained a Jesuit priest in 1911 and served as a chaplain in World War I. Early in his education, he was deeply moved by Henri Bergson's *Creative Evolution*, and the spiritual aspects of evolution would become a lifelong interest.

In 1923, he went to China for the first time and became a member of several anthropological expeditions there. He returned to China in 1926 and worked with the team that discovered Peking Man. During these years, his teaching and writing were repeatedly condemned by his religious superiors as giving too little attention to original sin. He composed the *Divine Milieu* and *The Phenomenon of Man* during the 1920s but was forbidden to publish them.

He visited the United States for the first time in 1930 and would return to New York in the 1950s. When he died in 1955, his longtime personal assistant Rhoda de Terra and others saw that his manuscripts were finally published.

1 Jacques Maritain, "The Christian and History," *Jubilee*, November 1957, 29.
2 Jacques Maritain, *Art and Scholasticism*, 6.
3 Maritain, 18.
4 *Pastoral Constitution on the Church in the Modern World (Gaudium et Spes)*, no.1, 163, 231.
5 Jacques Maritain, *The Range of Reason*, 165.
6 Maritain, *True Humanism*, xii.
7 Maritain.
8 Maritain.
9 Maritain, xiv.
10 Dupré, *The Passage to Modernity*, 33.
11 Dupré, 34.
12 Maritain, *True Humanism*, 66.
13 Wolfe, *Beauty Will Save the World*, quoting Virgil Nemoianu's vision of Christian humanism, 34.
14 O'Connor, *The Habit of Being*, 43.
15 O'Connor, 449.
16 A single unsigned page (p. 22), with accompanying full-page photo on p. 23, *Jubilee*, September 1959.
17 McCarty, 27.
18 O'Connor, *The Habit of Being*, 422.
19 Cardinal Christoph Schönborn, *Chance or Purpose? Creation, Evolution, and a Rational Faith*, 141.

Part Three

A World Enchanted—Again

In the course of the 1950s, American Catholics began to reimagine their place in the world: from a defensive *Church Militant* to a humbler *pilgrim people*. The publication *Jubilee,* launched in 1953, vigorously expressed an emerging ideal among Catholics: to "bridge the gap between religion and culture."[1]

During the 1960s, Catholic involvement in America's cultural life came into its own. With the election of John F. Kennedy as president, stereotypes of Catholics as not quite American fell silent. The Second Vatican Council (1962–65) deployed a new language of pluralism and an almost-forgotten sense of mystery that opened religious faith to new appreciations of enchantment, artistic and religious.

This era also saw a new interest in enchantment in science and literature. The writings of Rachel Carson, Annie Dillard, and Wendell Berry testify to this movement. Catholic authors such as Mary Gordon caught the contrast between an earlier Catholic imagination and the vision of faith emerging in the 1960s and '70s.

The four novels of Marilynne Robinson, written in the last decades of the century and the first years of the new century, and her celebration of "the rituals of the ordinary" represent a compelling literary venture in the enchantment of religious faith.

---

[1] Mary Anne Rivera, "Jubilee: A Magazine of the Church and Her People," *Logos: A Journal of Catholic Thought and Culture,* 98.

Chapter Nine
Anticipation—*Jubilee*
Magazine

CR

*To build a bridge of understanding out into secular culture
and to act as interpreters of the Christian faith to the world
outside the Church.*

—Mission statement of *Jubilee*

In 1953, a new Catholic journal, *Jubilee*, appeared in the land. Arriving nine years before the beginning of the Second Vatican Council, this monthly publication presaged a profound shift in the Catholic imagination. The first issue of *Jubilee*, a liberally illustrated thirty-five-cent monthly, was mailed to its first 10,000 charter subscribers in April of 1953. Pivoting from a more traditional posture of defensiveness and religious insularity, Ed Rice, the magazine's founder and first publisher, ambitioned a new optimism and enthusiasm that would place the Catholic Church in dialogue with its surrounding environment. *Jubilee* aspired to be, in the retrospective opinion of its publisher, "a significant force in the awakening of the American Catholic Church to a wider world in the postwar and Vatican II period."[1] The first article in the first issue was on "The Church and the Cold War" by John Cogley. It was followed by an article, with photos, on First Communion dresses and an ad for a new book by Bishop Fulton J. Sheen.

The magazine, with its emphasis on the "cheerfulness and joy" of everyday life—the title, *Jubilee*, referred to the biblical *Jubilate Deo omnis terra* ("Shout for joy to God, all the earth")—marked a decided turn from the more apologetic tone of earlier Catholic authors. In the same period that Evelyn Waugh was railing against the pagan world and Flannery O'Connor was complaining about the nihilism that permeated society, Rice and his colleagues Robert Lax and Thomas Merton were encouraging a confident engagement with the world around them. They wanted to publish a magazine that would help readers reorient themselves in a changing world and that would show the beauty and truth of the Catholic Church to the larger world. To do this, *Jubilee* began publishing articles about reforms in the liturgy that were just beginning.

Catholics Engaged—in the Liturgy

This shift in the Catholic imagination to a more optimistic engagement with culture would be complemented by a pivot from a faith life of private piety to one of communal celebration. For the laity, the Eucharist had become a private devotion, with individuals passively listening to the priest's incomprehensible prayers in Latin and others in the pews serving as little more than distraction to their individualistic piety. Flannery O'Connor, during her three years of study in Iowa in the late 1940s, recalled attending daily Mass at the nearby Catholic parish: "I went there three years and never knew a soul in that congregation or any of the priests, but it was not necessary. As soon as I went in the door I was at home."[2]

In 1951, two years before *Jubilee* was launched, liturgical renewal had begun with a return to the elaborate liturgy of the Easter vigil. In place of the customary Sunday Mass, Catholic parishes were now to gather the evening before Easter Sunday for a celebration that began in darkness outside the door of the church. The liturgical leader was to light a fire, and from this first illumination the Easter candle was lit and then the candles held by participants. The community entered the church, and as the candles illumined the darkened building, the celebrant intoned *lumen Christi* (the light of Christ).

This radical change in the Easter liturgy was intended to reclaim earlier traditions and to return enchantment to the central celebration of the liturgical year. Parishes and pastors, often awkwardly, struggled with this more complicated and seemingly novel style of worship. (As a twelve-year-old altar boy, I helped our pastor, Father Ketter, start a fire in a dilapidated barbecue pit outside the door of the church in the bitter cold of a Minnesota March night.)

Four years later, the Church instituted a wholesale reform of the liturgies of Holy Week. On Holy Thursday, the ancient ceremony of washing of feet, most often neglected or restricted to cathedrals, was to be practiced in every parish. On Good Friday, all Catholics, not just clergy, were encouraged to kiss the cross, instrument of Jesus's death. The tabernacle was then dramatically emptied and its doors left open to remind parishioners of Jesus's death. Again, the intent of this renewal was to return a sense of enchantment to Catholic worship, much of which had become, over centuries, both rote and private.

Theologian George Tavard provided readers of *Jubilee* with a theological rationale for a more communal vision of liturgy. "Christians do not receive the Lord by themselves in acts of private devotion."[3] The goal of the ongoing liturgical reform was to "recover the organic piety which [Catholics] have largely lost."[4] Tavard reminded readers that these changes were not novel interjections; "Our millennium-old liturgical texts are precisely meant to evoke an experience of intense fellowship."[5]

This call for a more active engagement in the liturgy was met, of course, by some resistance. A reviewer of Jacques and Raïssa Maritain's *Liturgy and Contemplation* in the August 1960 issue recalled the authors' "gently admonishing those misguided champions of corporate worship who seem to belittle mental prayer, all private devotions, silent adoration."[6] The Maritains argued in their book, according to the reviewer, that all "exterior public worship must be principally interior, since the love of God is always from person to person. *It is never a group activity.*"[7]

In the April 1956 issue, *Jubilee* reproduced the entire new liturgy for Holy Week that had been prepared by Godfrey Diekmann, O.S.B. And in the August 1958 issue, the magazine published a long photo essay on a parish in Minneapolis that showed the celebrant saying Mass while facing the congregation. This photo was both shocking and inviting: Could the liturgy be celebrated this way? The Catholic imagination began to stir.

As these changes, the fruit of a half century of research in Europe, were introduced, *Jubilee* threw itself into the task of overcoming the deep passivity in Catholics' attendance at liturgies. In the August 1955 issue, the editors of *Jubilee* published a survey on the use of the English Missal at Mass. Readers responded with enthusiasm about this new prayer book that helped them participate in the Mass more fully, now being able to follow the prayers of the Mass in their own language.

Catholics Engaged—in the Culture

Jubilee's mission was to encourage not only greater lay participation in the liturgy, but in the broader culture as well. The goal of the magazine was to "bridge the gap between religion and culture by bringing into view a new world in which it is the privilege of the Christian to cooperate with God in restoring all things to Christ."[8] *Jubilee* repeatedly advocated a vision of Christian life in which "Christianity is constantly being acted out in the daily lives of its people, in towns, cities, nations and continents."[9] It was not enough to "keep the faith," embracing it as a personal gift; Catholic were being called to "do the faith," expressing the good news of the faith to the wider world.

In issue after issue, *Jubilee* celebrated the many new channels of social engagement: Young Christian Workers gathered to seek justice in the workplace; the organization of Young Christian Students and the Christian Family Movement were both expanding their influence. The magazine ran articles on "Catholics and Democracy" and "Catholics and US Labor." These were suddenly seen as relevant to the life of faith. Articles on segregation and "Catholicism and the Negro" followed.

Other articles told the story in photos of a Presbyterian parish and of the Orthodox Church. Ecumenism, in its initial phase, became a new concern as Catholics were encouraged to see Protestants not as religious foes but as fellow believers. Here, too, the traditional Catholic imagination was expanding its boundaries.

Voices from Abroad

A major contribution of *Jubilee* magazine was the exposure of its readers to the exciting and challenging theology of European scholars. French Dominican Yves Congar made an appearance in the June 1957 issue with his essay on "The Layman, the Church and the World" in which he clarified the complementarity of interior piety and external witness of one's faith. "After having set the faithful apart from the world by His call, God puts them back into it and assigns to each a task and duty."[10]

Congar reminded readers that they are not to see themselves as exiles in an alien land. "We are pilgrims, travelers in the world, but we are not mere tourists."[11] He urged lay Christians to move beyond a sense of themselves as children and embrace the challenges of adults: engagement and responsibility. "There is much that needs doing to cure lay people of their mania for looking for directions that dispense them from thinking out their own problems, and to dissuade the clergy from their habit of deciding and prescribing for everything."[12]

Congar also introduced American Catholics to the notion of a religious humanism. "In a frenzied world, it is for them to pursue a long-term policy of true humanism, sanity and serious work, if they believe in

God wholeheartedly enough to believe in man as God believes in him."[13]

Like Congar, Romano Guardini emphasized a gentler image of the Creator with an essay on "The Patience of God."[14] Guardini, author of *The Lord* (published in an English translation in the late 1940s), pictured God not as the relentless pursuer of souls, impatient with human folly—the Catholic imagination we saw in Waugh and Greene—but as a God whose infinite compassion allows for the unfolding of grace in creation and in our lives. God, as the creator of time and its great swaths of history, "can therefore wait until the time is ripe—the time he has himself appointed."[15] Such a God, instead of reeling in souls "with a twitch of the thread" (Waugh), "allows things to develop quietly, freely, each thing in its own good time."[16]

And this divine patience is not only cosmic; God's patience defines the divine relationship with each of us. "God's patience is His patience with me. . . . If God takes as poor a view of me as I do myself, if God does not bear with my bungling, my dishonesty, my constant failures with greater patience than I do myself, then I am bound to give up in despair."[17] Guardini's style of writing—pastoral and compassionate—opened a refreshingly new approach to the faith. Flannery O'Connor repeatedly praised Guardini's writings, observing that: "in my opinion there is nothing like [his book, *The Lord*] anywhere, certainly not in this country."[18]

A Sea Change in the 1960s

With the death of Pius XII in 1958, the new pontiff, John XXIII, surprised everyone by calling for an ecumenical council. George Tavard, in an essay the following year, predicted a council that would invite laity into fuller participation in the liturgy as well as in lay apostolates in the world. All this, he hoped, would "prepare the end of the individualistic, devotions-centered piety which has too often replaced true liturgical and biblical worship."[19] Tavard also expressed his hopes that the Council would find ways to be linked to the World Council of Churches.

As the 1960s dawned, a new interest surfaced in the issues of *Jubilee*. In the September 1960 issue, an article on "The 'Divorced' Catholic" poignantly described the loneliness of a divorced man. The article showed great sympathy with his plight but raised no questions about any possibility of remarriage. In the July 1962 issue, John Todd wrote about "The Authority of the Layman," in which he argued that Church leaders should listen to lay Catholic experiences of marriage and sexuality. In the May 1963 issue, an article appeared on "Sex and the Teenager" by psychiatrist Robert Jean Campbell.

Two months later, Wilfrid Sheed wrote a supportive review of John Rock's book, *The Time has Come*. The title of the review was "Catholics and the Pill."[20] Dr. Rock was one of the early researchers on contraception and a devout Catholic. So began the debate, continuing today, on artificial birth control.

In 1964, the *National Catholic Reporter* published its first issue, and in the following years recruited many of *Jubilee's* readers. In August 1967, *Jubilee* suspended publication and in the following year agreed to merge with *U.S. Catholic*. Looking back, editor Rice described the shift in perspective that *Jubilee* had offered to American

Catholics. His words expressed the new direction that the Catholic imagination embarked on at midcentury. "The Church was dominated by 16th and 17th century Spanish pessimism in those days. . . . I thought this is not God. God is love. Priests are telling us that God punishes those He loves most. . . . that was wrong. God is your friend. We tried to reflect that in the magazine."[21]

1. Rivera, "Jubilee," 88.
2. Gooch, 121.
3. Tavard, "The Eucharist," *Jubilee*, June 1960, 8.
4. Tavard, 11.
5. Tavard.
6. Oona Sullivan, "Also of Interest," review of Jacques and Raïssa Maritain's *Liturgy and Contemplation*, *Jubilee*, August 1960, 44.
7. Sullivan.
8. Rivera, 98.
9. Rivera, 84.
10. Yves Congar, "The Layman, the Church and the World," *Jubilee*, June 1957, 17.
11. Congar, 19.
12. Congar.
13. Romano Guardini, "The Patience of God," *Jubilee*, May 1957, 16.
14. Guardini, 19.
15. Guardini, 18.
16. Guardini, 19.
17. Guardini.
18. O'Connor, *The Habit of Being*, 99.
19. Tavard, "The Eucharist," *Jubilee*, June 1960, 11.
20. Wilfred Sheed, "Catholics and the Pill: A Review of John Rock's *The Time has Come*," *Jubilee*, July 1963, 41.
21. Rivera, 100.

Chapter Ten
The Return of Enchantment

CR

*Our life is a faint tracing on the surface of mystery . . .
we must somehow take a wider view, look at the whole
landscape, really see it, and describe what's going on here.*

—Annie Dillard, *Pilgrim at Tinker Creek*

The aggiornamento announced in the Second Vatican Council threw open the windows on the world as Catholics took greater notice of what was transpiring beyond the confines of their religious communities. In its document on non-Christian religions, the Council acknowledged the common human effort to plumb the mystery of life. "Throughout history, to the present day, there is found among different peoples a certain awareness of a hidden power, which lies behind the course of nature and the events of human life."[1]

A new respect for such a *hidden power* reawakened in Catholics a celebration of the mystery at the heart of our world. This mystery—God's always-surprising grace—is the beginning of enchantment. The renewal sponsored by the Second Vatican Council turned attention to the charm of nature itself—the water, light, wind, and soil that sustain and enliven humans. God's grace, once sequestered in a transcendent realm beyond this world (*the supernatural*), was now recognized within the ordinary precincts of human life. This new attunement to nature was not rooted in a naïve prescientific appreciation of the cosmos, but in a postscientific reckoning with our mysterious world. Suddenly our world vibrates with enchantment.

In the years since the Council, Catholics have come to appreciate how this *hidden power* moves through the ordinary elements of water, oil, and bread as they are transfigured into sacraments of welcome in Baptism, of healing in the Anointing of the Sick (this term replacing Extreme Unction since 1972), and of nourishment in the Eucharist. Sacraments are exercises in sacred enchantment: the ordinary is transfigured into the extraordinary.

Water, blessed, becomes enchanted: *holy water*. Marilynne Robinson was onto this: in the novel *Gilead*, an aging pastor watches a couple delighting in rainwater sprinkling them as it spills from a tree branch. He muses, "It is easy to believe in such moments that water was made primarily for blessing, and only secondarily for growing vegetables or doing the wash."[2]

In the Eucharist, the celebrant invokes the Holy Spirit: "Make holy these gifts." Once prayed over, bread is broken and shared. In these actions, everyday nourishment is transfigured, becoming food of a whole other sort. This is a mystery, and a grace, and it is enchanting.

Assembled for a Good Friday liturgy, we gather with others around a large wooden cross. Each of us comes forward to touch with reverence this wood that is engrained with memories of Christ's suffering and our gratitude for the gift of his life. In this tactile expression of reverence, the cross is now enchanted.

Beyond these liturgical expressions, the everyday touches that bind parents and children and the loving embraces that bond marriage partners are made holy when performed with a similar reverence. These gestures evoke the *hidden power* that moves mysteriously to transfigure lives. The world teems with this potential: epiphanies of grace arise from the most ordinary interactions to enrich and heal wounded lives.

A Primitive Naïveté

Five hundred years ago, people everywhere saw their world through what Paul Ricoeur has described as the enchanted lens of "a primitive naïveté."[3] Shape-shifting transformations were an ordinary part of such a world. Spirits inhabited mountains and streams; heavenly deities regularly intervened in earthly matters. An eclipse of the sun or a devastating flood might signal divine displeasure. A child born blind could represent the moral failure of her parents. In such a world, it was all but impossible not to believe in the enchanting powers at play in human lives. In this era, enchantment kept company with magic and miracles, with alchemy and conjuring, with ghosts and their haunting presence.

For Jews and Christians, enchantment was to be found in every rainbow. The Creator, after nearly destroying the world with a flood, assured Noah that no such calamity would ever happen again. The rainbow that appeared in the sky after a storm was a divine guarantee of this promise. "I have set my bow in the clouds, and it shall be a sign of the covenant between me and the earth" (Genesis 9:12). Storm clouds giving way to this refreshing display: an enchanting gift of the Creator. The naïveté of this belief lay in the assumption that the Creator intervened in nature on each occasion to display a rainbow.

A Desert of Criticism

The unfolding of the modern world, with the advance of science and a growing trust in instrumental reason, brought with it a profound disenchantment. The animated *cosmos*—a place alive with signs and revelations—had been reduced to a physical *universe*—a world of mute matter guided not by God's hand but by mindless laws of physics. Science downsized the mysterious to the problematic; evolutionary biologist Edward O. Wilson said it well: "When we have unified enough certain knowledge, we will understand who we are and why we are here."[4]

Scientific rationalism confidently sought to solve questions that the human community had previously assumed were beyond fathoming. A comet was just a comet, not a heavenly signal. An eclipse of the sun bore no moral message. The drama of symbolic stories was replaced by a cool detachment of scientific research. The emotion of wonder, with its vital links to enchantment, was an early casualty: "By the late 16th century, European scientists began to look down on wonder; they began to see it as the mark of a childish mind, whereas the mature scientist went about coolly cataloging the laws of the world."[5] In this desert, the voices of Freud, Marx, and Nietzsche rang loudly and persuasively.

Magic and alchemy and the art of conjuring were casualties of this era, as was a familiarity with the ghosts who haunt everyday life. As these dynamics fell out of respectability, so did enchantment, victim of the company it kept.

A Second Naïveté

For many people today, this desert of criticism endures, with its sense that the world is only what we see and nothing more. Yet for many others, there remains an awareness, often tentative and unclear, that reality includes *more than meets the eye*. Many today are recovering a sense of the mystery in the world. Paradoxically, it is the very advance of science that is opening the door to a "second naïveté"—a humbler and more tentative style of believing.

The planet we inhabit—the charming "blue marble" displayed to us by circling astronauts—now seems to be more than mute matter running according to the rigid rules of physics. A more sophisticated appreciation of the natural world is provoking wonder at our planet's profound fragility, its extravagant immensity, and its mysterious interconnectedness.

In *Silent Spring*, Rachel Carson exposed the devastation that poisonous insecticides and other pollutants brought to streams and rivers, resulting in the deaths of wildlife and plant species. Her compelling descriptions stunned many into a new appreciation of the earth's fragility. Her reflections on the vital complexity of soil, the intricate balance of chemical and living organisms that renders fields fertile replaced a commonsense estimate of lifeless "dirt." The world was now reimagined not as a self-sufficient mechanism, but as a vulnerable organism.

Astronomers and cosmologists today describe a universe whose immensity is all but incomprehensible. We learn that there are now thought to be 100 billion galaxies. Our universe has existed for billions of years before we came on the stage. How to comprehend this vastness? Why is there so much? Or, perhaps the deeper wonder, why is there anything at all?

Scientists today are also calibrating the interconnectedness of all matter. The blood that flows through our veins contains the same iron that exists in the stars; the calcium in our bones is the same element found in the oceans. Biophysicist Tyler Volk has written about "the global metabolism" in which the exchange of oxygen and carbon dioxide, through photosynthesis, regulates the planet as a single breathing organism. Other scientists examine the extraordinary coincidences of chemistry that permit life on earth: constancy of temperature, the abundant availability of liquid water, the level of atmospheric oxygen that remains at 21 percent—the precise level required to sustain life. What to make of these "coincidences in our favor"? Appreciation and wonder seem our best response.

In the late modern world we inhabit today—what Ricoeur describes as *a second naïveté*—many have grown restless with an inherited mood of disenchantment. We are ready to name experiences of insight and grace that escape the iron cage of a disenchanted rationality. Having abandoned belief in literal magic, we are able to describe a play like *The Lion King* as magical. No longer believing in alchemy, we are willing to deploy the metaphor of alchemy to describe the fascinating dynamics of a friendship. Having rejected the literal reality of conjuring, novelist Marilynne Robinson can speak of all great art as an exercise in conjuring. When we no long adhere to ancient beliefs about ghosts, we are comfortable with John Lahr's question, "Can we agree that we're all haunted? The ghost world is part of our world. We carry within us the good and the bad, the spoken and unspoken imperatives of our missing loved ones."[6]

The Catholic imagination is extraordinarily capacious: it sustains, with some tension, a wide variety of convictions. In John's gospel alone, we glimpse this tension with the single word "world" (*cosmos*). Early in the gospel (3:16), we read that "God so loved the world." This belief makes the world lovable, even enchanting. Later in the gospel, Jesus warned his disciples "the world hates you" and "I have chosen you out of the world" (John 15:19). This is the same world, glimpsed now through a different lens. Such a view has seemed, for many believers, to endorse the world as disenchanted—emptied of the captivating charm suggested by the world that God finds lovable. A disenchanted world is a darkened place awaiting to be illumined by grace descending from above. The world that God is in love with is a world lit from within.

Catholics and the Enchantment of Nature

In his 2015 encyclical on the environment, *Laudato Si'*, Pope Francis gives expression to Catholic convictions about the links of enchantment and nature. The encyclical directs our attention repeatedly to our fragile Earth, cherished product of God's creation, reminding us that we are more than tourists on this enchanting planet. The Pope describes nature as "sister Earth"[7] and "a common home which God has entrusted to us."[8] This natural world would enchant us if only we had eyes to see: "From panoramic vistas to the tiniest living form, nature is a constant source of wonder and awe. It is also a continuing revelation of the divine."[9]

Again and again the Pope seeks to locate the human journey within this fragile world. "As believers, we do not look at the world from without, but from within, conscious of the bonds with which the Father has linked us to all things."[10] He writes repeatedly of the beauty of the world and its power to recruit our care for this vulnerable planet. And he links this sensual beauty with the sacraments. "Through our worship of God, we are invited to embrace the world on a different plane. Water, oil, fire and colors are taken up in all their symbolic power and incorporated in our act of praise."[11]

In this new perspective, natural light itself begins to take on new significance. In Marilynne Robinson's *Gilead*, an old minister is dazzled not by a ritual flame but by ordinary light. "I was struck by the way the light felt that afternoon. I have paid a good deal of attention to light, but no one could begin to do it justice. . . . It was the kind of light that rests on your shoulders the way a cat lies on your lap."[12]

For essayist Annie Dillard, light is never ordinary; it always arrives as gift. "The literature of illumination reveals this above all: although it comes to those who wait for it, it is always, even to the most practiced and adept, a gift a total surprise."[13]   And, "I cannot cause light; the most I can do is try to put myself in the path of its beam."[14]

An Extravagant Creation

Poets and philosophers have joined scientists in reimagining the natural world and its enchantments. Annie Dillard writes, "If the landscape reveals one certainty, it is that the extravagant gesture is the very stuff of creation. After the one extravagant gesture of creation in the first place, the universe has continued to deal exclusively in extravagances, flinging intricacies and colossi down aeons of emptiness, heaping profusions on profligacies with ever-fresh vigor. The whole show has been on fire from the word go."[15]

She concludes, "This, then, is the extravagant landscape of the world, given, given with pizzazz, given in good measure, pressed down, shaken together, and running over."[16] We come to realize that "the universe is not made in jest but in solemn, incomprehensible earnest. By a power that is unfathomably secret, and holy, and fleet. There is nothing to be done about it, but ignore it, or see."[17]

Environmentalist Wendell Berry has long exhibited a spiritual devotion to nature and its enchantments. In his essay "An Entrance to the World," he describes his brief sojourn in nature during a brief retreat from city life. For Berry, nature is "a wilderness that is beautiful, dangerous, abundant, oblivious to us, mysterious, never to be conquered or controlled or second guessed, or known more than a little."[18] He reflects, "I have come here to enact . . . the loneliness and the humbleness of my kind. I must see in my flimsy shelter, pitched here for two nights, the transience of capitols and cathedrals."[19]

Charles Taylor comments on this return of enchantment: "Do we not now experience wonder at the vast yet intricate universe and the manifold forms of life, at the very spectacle of the evolution of higher forms out of lower? Do we not find beauty in this?"[20] Taylor speaks of a "new cosmic imaginary . . . the sense that our thinking, feeling life plunges its roots into a system of such unimaginable depths, that consciousness can emerge out of this, fills them too with awe."[21] This new awareness of the world's richness and depth suggests that our age is far from collapsing into unbelief.

Columnist David Brooks has raised the question of enchantment as a human capacity that must be developed. Brooks warns that a modern, utilitarian culture has little time for enchantment. In his essay "The Devotional Leap," he contrasts web-based dating services (a disenchanted exercise in expedited "shopping for human beings") with the more spontaneous encounters that may lead one toward "taking the leap of enchantment."[22]

The challenge in our time, he argues, is to build the capacity for enchantment, especially through "humanism, religion and the humanities, which are the great instructors of enchantment."[23] In today's world, "this is . . . a countercultural act and a practical and fervent need."[24]

Annie Dillard shall have the last word. "It could be that God has not absconded (*Deus Absconditus* of Deism) but spread, as our vision and understanding of the universe have spread, to a fabric of spirit and sense so grand and subtle, so powerful in a new way, that we can only feel blindly of its hem."[25]

1   Vatican II, Declaration on the Relation of the Church to Non-Christian Religions, *Nostra Aetate*, no. 2.
2   Robinson, *Gilead*, 28.
3   Paul Ricoeur, *The Symbolism of Evil*, 351.
4   Edward O. Wilson, *Consilience*, 7.
5   Jonathan Haidt, *The Happiness Hypothesis*, 206.
6   Lahr, "Trapped in Time," 92.
7   Francis, *Laudato Si'*, no. 53.
8   *Laudato Si'*, no. 232.
9   *Laudato Si'*, no. 85.
10 *Laudato Si'*, no. 220.
11 *Laudato Si'*, no. 235.
12 Robinson, *Gilead*, 51.
13 Annie Dillard, *Pilgrim at Tinker Creek*, 11.
14 Dillard, 11.
15 Dillard.
16 Dillard, 148.
17 Dillard, 275.
18 Wendell Berry, "An Entrance to the World," *The Art of the Personal Essay: An Anthology from the Classical Era to the Present*, Phillip Lopate, 673.
19 Berry, 674.
20 Charles Taylor, "Disenchantment-Reenchantment," *Dilemmas and Connections*, 295.
21 Taylor, 296.
22 David Brooks, "The Devotional Leap," *The New York Times*, 25.
23 Brooks.
24 Brooks.
25 Dillard, 9.

Chapter Eleven
Now I Must Open the Jar of Ointment

*We must not deprive ourselves, our loved ones, of the luxury
of our extravagant affections.*

—Mary Gordon's *Final Payments*

Final Payments, Mary Gordon's 1978 novel, quite inten-
tionally charts the shift taking place in the Catholic imagination at midcentury. A young woman lives with her
widowed father whose faith is expressed in a clear and
forceful fashion: "he loved the sense of his own orthodoxy" and "he kept intact that interface between the
sacred and the secular."[1] His daughter Isabel, unable to
embrace the certainties of her father's faith and unwill-
ing to practice the pieties of the family's housekeeper,
Margaret, will struggle to find a more fitting expression
of her Catholic faith.

It is 1962: Isabel Moore is nineteen years old and her
father is a retired professor of medieval literature. She
had recently been dating David Lowe, a devoted student
of her father, and she recalled their going together to
West Side Story that year. But that was also the year that
her father caught them having sex in her family home.
Isabel was filled with shame and remorse, emotions
that only deepened when, three weeks after this trau-
matic event, her father had a debilitating stroke. Isabel

139

decides, in a lethal combination of guilt and devotion, to utterly devote herself to caring for her ailing father. This selfless act will become for her a kind of sanctuary where she will, for the next eleven years, dedicate herself to the father she has so offended and begin to pay down the debt to God for her sinfulness. And this shuttered life will also allow her to avoid the hazards of living in the larger world.

For more than a decade, she abides in this cloistered existence. And during this period, she has ample time to appreciate the distinctive shape of her father's Catholic faith. "He believed in hierarchies; he believed that truth and beauty could be achieved only by a process of chastening and exclusion." This was very much the Catholic imagination that served Waugh and Greene. Her father believed that "one did not look for happiness on earth; there was a glory in poverty."[2]

As a teacher of medieval literature, her father often praised western culture but had never gone to a museum, opera, or ballet. Isabel came to realize that "what he meant by Western Civilization was the Church."[3] And he was keenly attuned to the differences that divided Catholics from other Christians. Her father saw Thanksgiving as a Protestant holiday. But his family was Catholic "with a tradition that was rich and ancient and had nothing to do with cold, thin-blooded Puritans sitting down somewhere in New England."[4]

Professor Moore had no desire to move from the Irish Catholic pocket in Queens where he had always lived. "It was natural for him not to want to leave the neighborhood where the church was so predominant it did not need to be upheld."[5] At the same time, her father's faith was anything but pious. He said the Rosary and prayed to his favorite saints, but his spirituality was "manly, gladiatorial. No woman could ever have approached anything like it, for his relations with God had nothing of the lover about them, as a woman's inevitably have. He and God were fellow soldiers."[6]

Isabel herself had grown up in this spiritual climate. In the years of her Catholic grade school education, the nuns insisted that the girls, when going to Communion, would "fold our hands so that they were Gothic steeples, not a mess of immigrant knuckles."[7] Catholics in the 1950s were very much aware of their outsider status and often sought to disguise "the immigrant knuckles" that made that status too obvious.

With her father's passing, Isabel felt unmoored. She busied herself selling the family home, finding a job, and reconnecting with her friends Liz and Eleanor—childhood companions she had long ignored. She found herself indulging in a short-term affair with one man and then entering into a longer-term affair with Hugh, a married man with small children. Without the security of her former life of utter sacrifice, she indulged herself in this illicit relationship, trading selfless for selfish.

Amid this emotional turmoil, Isabel began to see the unconscious bargain she had made in devoting her life to her infirm father: in this self-erasing sacrifice, she "had bought sanctuary by giving up youth and freedom, sex and life."[8] This decade of devotion was, in fact, a faux enchantment: what appeared to be the utmost piety became a place of hiding from life. Paying down the debt of her sinfulness, she had gained the esteem of the parish and neighborhood. The family lawyer praises her: "You're a saint, Isabel, a saint of God."[9] But this sanctuary where her all-consuming devotion was played out was exacting its own price.

Deciding that she could not ask Hugh to leave his wife and family, Isabel fell back into what she knew: she retreated into a second sanctuary. She determined to do "the one pure act" that her confessor had suggested: to devote herself to caring for Margaret, the now-elderly woman who had been her family's housekeeper after Isabel's mother had died. In this new act of self-sacrifice she hoped to find the protected and predictable life she had known when caring for her father. Isabel determined to "love Margaret as God loves His creatures, impartially, imperious to their individual nature and thus incapable of being really hurt by them."[10] She would love without wanting anything in return. This would both serve as further penitence for earlier sins and would afford her a guarantee of a life beyond reproach.

Again, sanctuary described her choice: "Here I had built myself a sanctuary, covered over with approval, safe from chance."[11] In assuming, again, this devotional role, she would be able to see herself as good and would be making yet another *payment* in her search for redemption.

The Crisis of Holy Week

For months Isabel puts up with Margaret's harangues and criticism—all part of her sacrifice. Isabel's life reaches a crisis only when her former pastor, the alcoholic Father Mulcahy, comes to visit her on Monday of

Holy Week. His solicitude for her well-being and Margaret's endless needling both prod Isabel to finally begin to turn from this self-abusive life. After her pastor's visit, Isabel finds herself going back to the Church she had long ago abandoned to attend the ceremonies of Holy Week. She observes the ceremonial washing of feet on Holy Thursday and participates in the veneration of the cross on Good Friday. These sensual and sacred rituals trigger memories of Isabel bathing her crippled father, a delicate, sensual caring for flesh. She recalls shaving her father each morning. Memories flood back of the every-day touching, cleaning, holding of her crippled father. And, in all this, she remembers their shared laughter. The sensual, with its links with laughter and happiness, begins to edge her out of the protective shell of her sanctuary.

As she determines to abandon this second sanctuary, she remembers from her adolescence the gospel story of Mary pouring a jar of ointment over Jesus's feet. Judas had objected, but Jesus responded, "The poor you have always with you; but me you have not always." Now she realized "what Christ was saying, what he meant, was that the pleasures of that hair, that ointment, must be taken. Because the accidents of death would deprive us soon enough. We must not deprive ourselves, our loved ones, of the luxury of our extravagant affections. We must not try to second-guess by refusing to love the ones we loved in favor of the anonymous poor." So she realized, "I knew now I must open the jar of ointment. I must open my life."[12]

Isabel now sees that her would-be devotion to Margaret and the pseudo-selfless love it entailed was anything but holy. In plunging her whole life, again, into this sanctuary of devotion, she had thought to hide from the perils and confusing pleasures of a genuine life.

Gordon makes clear, with hints throughout the novel, that Isabel's struggles were being played out on the terrain of her own body. Devoting herself first to her father, she had tried to ignore her body. In her months living with Margaret, she had allowed herself to gain weight; what did it matter? She had subjected herself to a terrible haircut, abandoning the long hair she had once loved. "And I had cut my hair. I had wanted to give up all I loved so that I would never lose it. I had tried to kill all that had brought me pleasure so that I would not be susceptible."[13] Now she became aware of the body that she had long neglected. The body can change: hair grows back and weight can be shed. She sensed her body becoming more alive, more attentive to the world around her. "I was light now, my body was high again, and dexterous, and clever."[14]

In the final act of this drama, Isabel decides to give the $20,000 from the sale of her family's home to Margaret—money that Margaret could use to support herself and hire needed help. This would be Isabel's *final payment* in her long effort to exorcise her guilt. On Holy Saturday evening, she calls her friends, who hurry to rescue her from her sanctuary. When Liz and Eleanor arrive, they laugh at her atrocious haircut. Then, "the three of us laughed. It was a miracle to me, the solidity of the joke. Even the cutting edge of it was a miracle. And our laughter was solid."[15] As they set out together, Isabel gives thanks: "For they had come the moment I called them, and they were here beside me in the fragile and exhilarating chill of the first dawn."[16] This was the dawn when Holy Week gave way to Easter.

The Company of Women (1980)

In her second novel, Gordon returns to familiar territory: the stark contrast between the Catholic spirituality that reigned in the first half of the twentieth century and the style of belief that emerged after Vatican II. The story she tells is of five women in their fifties and sixties who share as confessor and guru a priest, Father Cyprian, who is also in his sixties. The jewel of the story is Felicitas, the teenage daughter of Charlotte, one of the women. The women and Father Cyprian share a full-hearted devotion for this young woman in whom they find "their only hope."[17] Gordon suggests this exaggerated attention may be yet another faux enchantment as the priest and older women pour their devotion over this young girl.

Felicitas, born at midcentury, represents a Catholic imagination that is starkly different from that of her elders. "Her soul she saw as glass filled with sky and water, as beautiful, as light, as silvery and important."[18] Felicitas envisioned "the side of God apart from punishment, or care. The God that breathed, breathed over all."[19] Such images of God stand in stark contrast to the pursuing, truculent God portrayed in the novels of Waugh and Greene.

The Catholic imagination alive in Felicitas and the Catholic imagination that the old priest had absorbed decades earlier were bound to come into conflict. When Felicitas and Father Cyprian are walking around a farm, she picks a handful of grass and marvels at its sensuous smell, comparing it to the smell of heaven. Father Cyprian is scandalized and sets out to disabuse the girl of her love of the sensual. "In heaven there are no smells."[20] He forces her to smell the excrement of various farm animals until she finally vomits. Triumphant, he reminds her that "nature could trap. You could wander among sweet grasses and not think of God. You could mistake the grass for God, the fragrance." He ends his instruction: "You must hate the world and love God. And you must not be womanish."[21] Nature, the world, and women: In this passage, Gordon visits the enduring sources of suspicion in the Catholic imagination that still predominated at midcentury.

In this same section, Gordon recalls the liturgical reforms of that era. Despite the turn to the vernacular in the liturgy, Father Cyprian had received permission from the bishop to say a Latin Mass. He and his women friends regret the change to vernacular.

Charlotte: "There's nothing like a Latin mass, I always say."

"English is not a spiritual language," Father Cyprian adds. "It's the language of merchants."[22]

In part three of the novel, Felicitas is once again among the company of women, but now with the child she had out of wedlock seven years before. She is reconciling her life and her motherhood with her own daughter, Linda, and finding a new relationship with the aging priest, Father Cyprian. These final reconciliations are registered in the key of laughter. Throughout these two novels, Gordon returns again and again to the central themes of false sanctuaries, the elusive nature of happiness, and laughter as code for grace.

Sanctuaries That Protect;
Sanctuaries That Hide

Gordon makes special use of the notion of sanctuary that is so important in the Catholic imagination. We met this image first in *Brideshead Revisited* as Evelyn Waugh emphasized the symbolic role of the sanctuary lamp as sign of Christ's presence in this sacred space. In Catholic faith, the sanctuary was the most holy part of the church interior, the space reserved for the celebration of the Mass.

In medieval times, a church building might serve as sanctuary in another sense: a protected space for a fugitive in flight from civil authorities. In recent decades, a "sanctuary movement" appeared in Christian churches near the US border with Mexico as places where refugees from Central America might find protection. As President Trump wages war against immigrants, a number of American cities have declared themselves "sanctuary cities."

Gordon turns this Christian image on its head to describe, in *Final Payments*, the space into which Isabel has retreated. Devoting herself entirely to care for her father, she creates a sanctuary that marks her life as pious while shielding her from any of the challenges and vulnerabilities of social existence.

In her next novel, Gordon returns to this metaphor. Muriel, one of the older women in *The Company of Women*, pictures her own solitude and her devotion to Father Cyprian in this light. "She had brushed out with fire all the root connections of her life; she had kept clean for him and God, a sanctuary perfect in its stillness."[23] Sanctuaries, it turns out, are as ambiguous as any other human artifact: sacred spaces reserved for worship of God, or hiding places to protect one from the rigors of everyday life.

Laughter as the Last Word

In both of Gordon's novels, laughter has the last word. In the last pages of *Final Payments*, Isabel has set aside her sanctuaries and entered wholeheartedly into life with all its vulnerabilities. And she did this with her women friends, feeling the richness of their companionship. In a final scene, her women friends laugh at her atrocious hair-cut (residue of an earlier piety), but their laughter enfolds and enheartens Isabel. "And our laughter was solid."

In *The Company of Women*, Gordon highlights two very different kinds of laughter. As Father Cyprian and his farmer friend "teach" Felicitas about the noxious odors of animal excrement, their mocking laughter seers Felicitas's soul. Humiliated, "Felicitas would always remember that laugh. In that laugh she was the other, she would know always in that laugh what it was to be the outsider." And for years to come she "vowed never to forgive the force, the laughter."[24]

As the novel comes to its conclusion, Felicitas and Father Cyprian are reconciled with one another and Felic-itas observes, "I began noticing things in the world that made me laugh." And, "I began to laugh at my mother's jokes."[25] With Cyprian, from whom she had been alien-ated, now "we laughed as we hadn't laughed in years. We got back what we were both afraid we had lost forever: our great pleasure in each other." Now at last, "Our laugh-ter met, our words clicked like champagne glasses."[26]

As the novel concludes, Felicitas' daughter looks out the window at her mother and grandmother: "They are laughing." She rushes out to be with them; her mother picks her up, and she sees "my grandmother is laughing."[27]

Afterthoughts

Mary Gordon, born in 1949, is a cradle Catholic who was in her early teens during the Second Vatican Council. Her father died when she was seven years old; only later did she learn about his Jewish heritage, coming to terms with his life in the memoir, *The Shadow Man: A Daughter Searches for her Father*. Her first two novels were *Final Payments* (1978) and *The Company of Women* (1980).

In her essay, "Getting Here from There: A Writer's Reflections on a Religious Past," in *Good Boys and Dead Girls and other Essays,* Gordon's reflections are all enchantment. "I did want to be a nun. . . . I wanted to be beautifully kneeling in light, my young, straight back clothed in the magic garment of the anointed."[28] And with the ideal of sanctity: "I was not supposed to even strive to be popular, successful, beloved, or valued by the world. I was supposed to be a saint."[29] And with the liturgies of Holy Week: "the black vestments, the stripped altar, the shocking silence of the congregation, and then the midnight fire and the morning promise of Easter."[30]

Gordon is currently McIntosh Professor in English and Writing at Barnard College. She lives in New York with her husband Arthur Cash. They have two children, Anna and David.

[1] Gordon, *Final Payments,* 4, 12.
[2] Gordon, 4.
[3] Gordon, 11.
[4] Gordon, 187.
[5] Gordon, 11.
[6] Gordon, 40.
[7] Gordon, 9.
[8] Gordon.
[9] Gordon, 45.
[10] Gordon, 251.
[11] Gordon, 239.
[12] Gordon, 289.
[13] Gordon, 289.
[14] Gordon, 296.
[15] Gordon, 297.
[16] Gordon.
[17] Mary Gordon, *The Company of Women,* 7.
[18] Gordon, 6.
[19] Gordon.
[20] Gordon, 42.
[21] Gordon, 45.
[22] Gordon, 175.
[23] Gordon, 72.
[24] Gordon, 44.
[25] Gordon, 255.
[26] Gordon, 256.
[27] Gordon, 292.
[28] Mary Gordon, "Getting Here from There: A Writer's Reflections on a Religious Past," *Good Boys and Dead Girls and Other Essays,* 166.
[29] Gordon, 167.
[30] Gordon, 169.

Chapter Twelve
Rituals of the Ordinary

CR

"How oddly holiness situated itself among the things of the world."

—Marilynne Robinson, *Home*

Like Mary Gordon, novelist Marilynne Robinson celebrates the enchantment to be found in everyday life. To do this, Robinson focuses on what she terms "rituals of the ordinary."

In her first novel, *Housekeeping*, we are introduced to a widow and her children as they see to the household tasks of everyday life. The widow, still wearing the black of mourning, carries just-washed sheets outside, hanging them up to dry in the wind and sunshine. Robinson describes such actions as "performing the rituals of the ordinary as an act of faith." In the midst of such ordinary activity, "the wind that billowed her sheets announced to her the resurrection of the ordinary."[1] The ordinary task of washing sheets—and relying on the wind and sun to dry them—prepares these sheets to once again enfold the family in comfort and sleep.

In this same novel, the widow reflects on her intimacy with her three small daughters after their father's death. "Never since they were small children had they clustered about her so, and never since then had she been so aware of the smell of their hair, their softness, breathiness, abruptness."[2] This intimacy, both sensual and spiritual, filled her with a deep delight as she recalled times when one of her nursing infants would fasten her eyes on her mother's face while reaching for her other breast, or hair or lips, hungry to touch. This celebration of parenthood where the sensual and spiritual daily intertwine resonates with enchantment.

Catholic ethicist Cristina Traina recalls similar experiences: "What is the quality of the experience of exhaustedly, helplessly nestling a finally sleeping newborn in the crook of one's neck, rocking by a window at dawn? Of nursing a too-hungry infant at a too-full breast after a stressful day?" Traina concludes, "These may not be moments of pure selflessness, or of sexual arousal, but they are benevolent and they are erotic."[3]

For Robinson, holding children close and cleansing bed linens enact enchantments of everyday life. Such rituals of the ordinary celebrate the sacramental character of life.

Water, Light, and Laughter in a World Enchanted

In her second novel, *Gilead,* Robinson continues her exploration of the everyday force of water as contributing to rituals of the ordinary. Reverend John Ames, a central figure in the small town of Gilead, Iowa, recalls how when he was young, his grandfather came upon him and his friend as they were playing by the river. The old man scooped up a hatful of water and spilled it over the boys. He remembers the water billowing in the air before it fell on them. The old man walked away, leaving the boys "standing there in that glistening river, amazed at ourselves and shining like the apostles. I mention this because it seems to me transformations just that abrupt do occur in this life."[4]

Robinson returns repeatedly to the enchanting role of water. The old minister observes his young son and friend hopping around in a sprinkler and marvels at the transformation of water that the sprinkler achieves. This experience then triggers a memory of baptism in a stream.

Robinson's most emphatic celebration of water and the ritual of the ordinary appears in yet another memory that Ames cherishes. He had stopped on his way to church one morning to watch a young couple walking ahead of him in the street: "The sun had come up brilliantly after a heavy rain, and the trees were glistening and very wet." He notices that the young man, for whatever reason, jumped up and caught hold of a branch, causing the branch to pour water on the couple, who laughed and ran from the raining tree. Ames reflect that seeing a sight like that made it "easy to believe in such moments that water was made primarily for blessing, and only secondarily for growing vegetables or doing the wash."[5]

For Catholic readers, this episode echoes the liturgical practice when the celebrant begins the Eucharistic celebration by moving through the congregation sprinkling parishioners with water, reenacting the prayer of Psalm 51: "Sprinkle me with a hyssop branch and I will be made clean." This religious ritual enchants only if it resonates with the charming play of water in everyday life. Disconnected from those memories, such a religious ceremony may appear as little more than magic.

Natural light, like water, serves as occasion of enchantment. The minister was often struck by the way sunlight fell on an afternoon. Light had a certain weight: "It was the kind of light that rests on your shoulders the way a cat lies on your lap." Ames later wonders at the light of the moon: "The moon looks wonderful in this warm evening light, just as a candle flame looks beautiful in the light of morning. Light within light. It seems like a metaphor for something."[6]

Joining water and light in Robinson's vision of the ordinary gracefulness of nature is laughter. The wet branch sprinkling the couple evoked a laugh of delight. John Ames wonders at the sheer beauty of people breaking into laughter. As he watched two young men joking around, he mused, "It is an amazing thing to watch people laugh, the way it sort of takes them over. . . . So I wonder what it is and where it comes from, and I wonder what it expends out of your system, so that you have to do it till you're done."[7]

As Ames looks back at the dizzying experience of falling in love—especially as an older man falling for a younger woman—he reflects, "At that point I began to suspect, as I have from time to time, that grace has a grand laughter in it."[8] Laughter may measure the enchanting presence of grace.

Visions and Enchanting Memories

"Your old men shall dream dreams, and your young men shall see visions."

The prophet Joel's prediction about dreams and visions (Joel 2:28) alerts us to the possibility of seeing beyond the obvious and the everyday to realities that exist just beyond our gaze. In *Gilead*, Robinson provides a striking reinterpretation of this capacity and gift. John Ames, writing to his young son, recalls how his own grandfather, also a minister, had spoken of the visions in which the Lord would appear to him when they would converse. "When I was a young man the Lord came to me and put His hand here on my right shoulder . . . would call that experience a vision. We had visions in those days, a number of us did."[9]

Ames realizes that he himself is not privileged with such supernatural visitations. Yet something similar to these visions comes to him in certain cherished memories. He returns to just such a memory of the time that a church, struck by lightning, had burned to the ground. Families from the area had gathered to pull down the remains of the building and rescue a few Bibles and hymnals that had survived the fire. The pews in the church, he recalls, "were mostly kindling." Yet the pulpit had somehow survived intact, so they put it under a tree and covered it with a blanket. The burned Bibles and prayer books they gathered and buried near the church, one grave for the ruined Bibles, and one for the prayer books.

Ames recalls that the mood of the day was almost like a camp meeting as people arrived from all over. And he remembers the children playing on blankets and the women setting out the food they had brought, and the rain that suddenly arose, and the people simply putting up with the soaking as they went about their work.

He remembers the men who were working in the ashes of the church and how the ash turned into mush in the rain. He recalls his father bringing him a biscuit that had soot on it. When he seemed bothered by the ash, his father assured him, "Never mind . . . there's nothing cleaner than ash." In his memory, bread and ash mingle and are accompanied by a powerful sense of communion. "I remember it as communion, and I believe that's what it was."[10]

Some cherished memories return as revelation, igniting in us a depth of emotion that exceeds our full apprehension. Memory itself, at the edge of our consciousness and not always under our bidding, transfigures the ordinary to reveal and "sanctify" the everyday as exceptional. Robinson's example of a sooty biscuit taken as communion reiterates her conviction that sacredness appears in the most ordinary parts of life. This, too, is part of what she had described in *Housekeeping* as "the rituals of the ordinary." Now, when Ames holds a Bible in his hand, he often recalls that scene at the destroyed church building, and the Bible "is somehow sanctified by that memory."[11] The sacred book does not sanctify the memory but quite the opposite: the memory makes holy the Bible.

The charming world that Ames' grandfather had inhabited (enjoying direct communication with the Lord) was no more, but another kind of enchantment had survived. Memories of sooty biscuits become spiritual communion testify to a world still open to enchantment. Paul Ricoeur would describe the grandfather's literal "visions" in terms of a *primitive naïveté*, an immediacy of belief, now lost. But in its place Robinson and Ames, in a *second naïveté*, find another kind of enchanting vision. Spiritual "visions" continue to exist, now encased in compelling memories. This, too, is an example of what Robinson calls the rituals of the ordinary.

Rituals of the Ordinary and the Novel *Home*

In her third novel, *Home,* Robinson tells the story of John Ames' closest friend, minister Jack Boughton and his two adult children, Glory and Jack. Returning home at age thirty-eight to care for her ailing father, Glory finds the old house is no longer a home for her. "What does it mean to come home? Glory had always thought home would be a house less cluttered and ungainly than this one, in a town larger than Gilead, or a city, where someone would be her intimate friend and the father of her children, of whom she would have no more than three."[12]

She faces the realization that this dream will not come to pass. "She knew, she had known for years, that she would never open a door to that home, never cross that threshold, never scoop up a pretty child and set it on her hip and feel it lean into her breast and eye the world from her arms with the complacency of utter trust. Ah well." Glory reflects on how care for her father was the shape of her faith now. "Faith for her was habit and family loyalty, a reverence for the Bible which was also literary, admiration for her mother and father. And then that thrilling quiet of which she had never felt any need to speak."[13]

The Prodigal Son

Jack, her older brother, has been gone for twenty years and has now returned to visit the ailing father and try to come to terms with his own wandering. In his misspent youth, he had fathered a child with a young girl, then left town. On his return, it is learned that Jack had later married an African-American woman and had another child—that they lived in poverty due to his alcoholism and inability to hold a job.

Glory remembers the restlessness of Jack as a boy. "There was an aloofness about him more thoroughgoing than modesty or reticence. It was feral and fragile. . . . Why would a child have defended his loneliness that way? He'd smile at them across that distance, and the smile was sad and hard, and it meant estrangement, even when he was with them." Jack never quite belonged to the family; "He was the black sheep, the ne'er-do-well. . . . It was the sad privilege of blood relations to love him despite all."[14]

Even in Jack's youth, his parents and siblings "were so afraid they would lose him, and then they had lost him, and that was the story of their family, no matter how warm and fruitful and robust it might have appeared to the outside world."[15]

Robinson in this novel is retelling the biblical parable of the prodigal son. In the New Testament we read of an alienation of father and son overcome. Here we read a sadder story: even when Jack had returned home, he could not let himself belong again to his family and birthplace. At the end of the novel Jack, who is a puzzle to himself, has left home once again. Glory allows herself to believe that "if he ever came to any of them he would be deeply and immediately welcome, however disreputable he might seem or be."[16]

Out of Exile: The Ordinary as Miraculous

In her fourth novel, *Lila*, Robinson introduces us to the young woman who, after a homeless, wandering youth—surviving as a veritable wild child—rather miraculously shows up in Gilead and eventually marries the old pastor Ames, who is now seventy years old.

Prior to her life in Gilead, Lila was a homeless waif, rescued by another wandering woman named Doll. The two of them traveled in a troupe of homeless vagabonds, just surviving at the edge of society. After Doll is injured in a knife fight and is jailed, Lila sets out on her own, working for a time in a house of prostitutes in St. Louis, and finally coming to rest in an abandoned shack just outside the small town of Gilead.

On occasion she wanders curiously into the town, even going into the church where old John Ames is the minister. Later, she tends the garden behind his house and cares for the cemetery plot where Ames's young wife, who died in childbirth decades ago, is buried. As the old pastor feels greater and greater affection for this young, untamed woman, they exchange hesitant conversation. In time and against the odds they come together, marry, and have a son. It is to this young son that the aging minister, John Ames, writes the memoir/letter that forms Robinson's second novel, *Gilead*.

In *Lila*, Robinson returns to her favorite themes of water and laughter. When Lila was still a homeless child, she wandered under the protection of Doll, an older woman who would give the girl some water to drink and then dip "her fingers into the cup to wet them and rinse dust from the child's face. Cold drops ran down her chin and throat and into the damp of her dress, and she laughed."[17] Again, the laughter that accompanies the ordinary grace of water.

Later, when Lila is bunking down in the shack near Gilead, she would wash her dresses in the river. "When she lifted them out [of the water], held them up to their shoulders, they looked like pure weariness and regret. But when she hung them over a line and let the water run out, and the sun and the wind dry them, they began to seem like things that could live."[18] As in the novel, *Housekeeping*, the ritual of the ordinary—sun and wind drying wet clothes—does its magic. Yet later in the novel, Lila considers presenting herself for baptism. "She thought there might be something about the water on her forehead that would cool her mind."[19]

When the child of Ames and Lila is born, a winter storm is raging in Gilead. Ames goes outside the house and gathers up some snow to melt for the child's baptism. "It was for christening the child, she knew without asking. If the child came struggling into the world, that water would be ready for him. If it had to be his only blessing, then it would be a pure and lovely blessing."[20] Snow transformed into water; water transformed into a ritual of blessing.

A theme running through Robinson's first novel is the enduring tension between the daily, repeated tasks of housekeeping and the experience of transience. The story begins with sensual descriptions of housekeeping, but when the children's mother dies and a shiftless aunt arrives, housekeeping is abandoned as the two children and their Aunt Sylvie exist in an increasingly cluttered and uncared for house. When neighbors notice the group's eccentricity (riding a freight train, for instance) and the community moves to have the sole remaining daughter, Ruthie, removed, Aunt Sylvie and Ruthie make a last-minute stab at housekeeping—but it is too late, so they flee the town for a life of wandering. Robinson announces: "Now truly we were cast out to wander, and there was an end to housekeeping."[21]

In the novel *Home,* the tension shifts: now it exists between the comforts of home and exile. Glory reflects on the romantic ideals of home that fit neither her life nor that of her prodigal brother, Jack. "Home. What kinder place could there be on earth, and why did it seem to them all like exile?"[22] In her fourth novel, *Lila,* Robinson shifts again to the theme of Lila's wandering and her hope for a home life. Even when she has married John Ames, Lila harbors thoughts of needing to return to her wandering days. Only at the end of this novel does Robinson allow herself a hopeful view of how all these tensions might ultimately be healed.

Enchantments of Love and Prayer

Falling in love—that most common, most natural place where the sensual and the spiritual join forces—evokes for John Ames a wonderment. Robinson details with loving care the minister's musing on the overthrownness of falling in love, the sense of the ridiculous, of the vulnerability of this experience. "For the first time in my life I felt I could be snatched out of my character, my calling, my reputation, as if they could just fall away like a dry husk." He turns to Scripture, reads in the Song of Songs "I am sick with love," and reflects, "It makes me laugh to remember this."[23] Again, laughter registers the inbreaking of grace.

As the old minister muses on his love of Lila, he admits to himself that he is comparing "love of God with mortal love. But I just can't see them as separate things at all. If we can be divinely fed with a morsel and divinely blessed with a touch, then the terrible pleasure we find in a particular face can certainly instruct us in the nature of the very grandest love."[24]

Lila, new to the world of religion, wonders what her husband is doing when he prays. "She meant to ask him sometime how praying is different from worrying." He had once described it as "troubling heaven." Robinson suggests we see prayer as one more ritual of the ordinary. The old preacher says, "*Family* is prayer. *Wife* is prayer. *Marriage* is prayer."[25] These ordinary words, with their associations of love and worry, might as well be prayers.

Robinson's novels display a sacramental vision of reality: the sensual as portal to the spiritual. Grace is not imported from another, supernatural realm to clean or cover over a soiled world, but abides within this world—sparkling in water and light and laughter—where home and exile will constantly contend for human hearts. Glory, reading the Bible, reflects on the mystery of this enchanted world: "How oddly holiness situated itself among the things of the world, how endlessly creation wrenched and strained under the burden of its own significance."[26]

Afterthoughts

In a number of essays, Robinson has sought to explain her goals as a Christian novelist. "As a writer, I continuously attempt to make inroads on the vast terrain of what cannot be said—or said by me, at least. I seem to know by intuition a great deal that I cannot find the words for, and to enlarge the field of my intuition every time I fail again to find these words. That is to say, the unnamed is overwhelmingly present and real for me."[27]

Literary critics have noticed how "Robinson insists on portraying virtuous characters who are also interesting—a difficult challenge in modern literature." Joan Acocella adds, "Ames is a kind of character that people say novelists can't create, an exceptionally virtuous person who is nevertheless interesting."[28]

In a review of Robinson's *Lila*, Diane Johnson salutes the author: "It is courageous of Robinson to write about faith at a time when associations with religion are so often negative or violent." Johnson adds, "And goodness . . . is even harder than piety to convey without succumbing to the temptation to charge it with sanctimony or hypocrisy."[29]

Robinson, in her nonfiction essays, returns often to her Calvinist roots. She understands her fiction to be portrayals of Calvin's optimism about the wonder of God's creation. Despite this embrace of Calvinism, Robinson blithely rejects two of its central tenets: the predestination of the elect for salvation and the "utterly corrupt" nature of humans.

Predestination for Robinson "is a classic instance of an inquiry beyond human capacity, which has multiplied disputes and confirmed skepticism, and has distorted Christianity as often as the doctrine is embraced or evaded."[30] As to Calvin's convictions about human nature being "utterly corrupt": "Calvin's sense of human depravity, however honestly come by, is by far the most conventional aspect of his thought." She adds, "He is unique, as far as I can tell, in rescuing out of the general ruin the whole human being, body, mind, and spirit."[31] Calvin's understanding of this "depravity" is anything but conventional; it dogs many Christians today, leading them to distrust the movements of their own hearts.

Robinson's genius is her ability to "feel the sanctity of the bonds we think we cherish [that] open onto the inarticulable richness concealed in the garments of the ordinary."[32] This vision is deeply sacramental; Robinson is as much Catholic as she is Calvinist.

Robinson comes closest to this book's theme of enchantment when she observes, "All our best art is the art of conjurers, calling up likenesses, inviting recognition, their praise and vindication being that they may have made something true to life."[33]

[1] Marilynne Robinson, *Housekeeping*, 17–18.
[2] Robinson, 11.
[3] Cristina Traina, *Erotic Attunement*, 65.
[4] Robinson, *Gilead*, 203.
[5] Robinson, 28.
[6] Robinson, 51, 119.
[7] Robinson, 5.
[8] Robinson, 207.
[9] Robinson, 175.
[10] Robinson, 96
[11] Robinson, 96.
[12] Robinson, *Home*, 102
[13] Robinson, 110.
[14] Robinson, 69.
[15] Robinson, 66.
[16] Robinson, 311.
[17] Robinson, *Lila*, 14.
[18] Robinson, 78.
[19] Robinson, 34.
[20] Robinson, 245.
[21] Robinson, *Housekeeping*, 209.
[22] Robinson, *Home*, 282.
[23] Robinson, *Gilead*, 204.
[24] Robinson.
[25] Robinson, 237.
[26] Robinson, *Home*, 102.
[27] Robinson, *When I Was a Child I Read Books*, 20.
[28] Joan Acocella, "Lonesome Road," *The New Yorker*, 80.
[29] Diane Johnson, "Moral of the Story," *The New York Times*, 12.
[30] Robinson, *The Givenness of Things*, 192–93.
[31] Robinson, 228.
[32] Robinson, 223.
[33] Robinson, 235.

Epilogue
A World Lit from Within

෴

"Wherever you turn your eyes the world can shine like transfiguration."

—Marilynne Robinson, *Gilead*

The Christian story begins in an enchanted garden, "the Lord God walking in the garden at the time of the evening breeze" (NRSV). We have seen Evelyn Waugh's novel *Brideshead Revisited* drawing on this metaphor. The young Charles Ryder reflected, "I was in search of love in those days, and I went full of curiosity and the faint, unrecognized apprehension that here, at last, I should find that low door in the wall, which others, I knew, had found before me, which opened on an enclosed and enchanted garden."[1]

Thomas Merton described his Trappist vocation as the entry into a wintry garden. He wrote of that fateful day in December 1941: "Brother Matthew locked the gate behind me and I was enclosed in the four walls of my new freedom. And it was appropriate that the beginning of freedom should be as it was. For I entered a garden that was dead and stripped and bare."[2] Merton savored the paradox that a winter garden, stripped and bare, would be the setting in which he would seek and find his spiritual enchantment.

Novelist Tessa Hadley reflects on the charm of the book "The Secret Garden" that she had read in childhood. This is the story of a young girl living in a big house on the Yorkshire moors with her uncle. The uncle "is reclusive and embittered because his wife was killed in an accident in a garden—the garden is locked now, so no one can get inside." Returning to this book as an adult, Hadley can see the social class values running through this novel published in 1911. "Yet even while I'm decoding all this, I'm still enthralled."

Hadley muses, "Looking around with adult eyes, I suppose that I can see over the top of the wall of the secret garden: I can see the ideological underpinnings, understand the context, sniff out the falsities. And yet . . . submission is stronger." Hadley recognizes the gap between the analytic adult in her and the child still abiding within: "My doubting, critical self seems smaller, moving around inside the novel's spaces, than the believing child who was here first. It's the adult who feels dwarfed and tiny within the huge shape of the child's experience."[3] The adult in us knows that "secret gardens" do not exist; yet the child in us still believes in such enchanted spaces. "Unless you change and become like children." (Matthew 18:3 NRSV).

In *Housekeeping*, Robinson was thinking of gardens. If humans are transients moving through history, we are journeying not as exiles ever further away from an original garden, but toward a final resting place—awaiting "a garden where all of us as one will sleep in our mother Eve."[4]

At the close of this same novel, Robinson allows herself an extended metaphor that is not far from that of a garden to capture the gracious resilience that is seeded into our everyday existence. She imagines the wounded world as like "Carthage sown with salt," referring to the Romans' destruction of the North African city and their effort to render it forever infertile. But even such efforts of annihilation cannot succeed. After many decades the soil of Carthage managed to dilute and then overcome the salt's toxicity. Triumphant over an earlier destruction, vegetation grew again. Such deep-down resilience is but one aspect of the earth's enchantment. Robinson concludes this meditation: "And here again is a foreshadowing—the world will be made whole."[5]

Ashes to Ashes: How Enchantment Works

The story of this book began with T. S. Eliot's transfiguration of the "dust" of *The Waste Land*, which registered Europe's disenchantment after World War I, into the enchanted ashes of the Catholic ritual at the beginning of Lent (*Ash Wednesday*). This was our first lesson in the play of enchantment. Near the story's end, we met Marilynne Robinson returning to this metaphor of ashes. In *Gilead*, John Ames recalls the powerful memory of his father offering him a biscuit tinged with ash as their family helped respond to a church that has just burned down. The boy is at first put off by the dirty bread, but his father assures him, "there's nothing cleaner than ash."

As Ames reflects on this compelling moment with his father, he thinks of the phase "bread of affliction," recalling the unleavened bread that the Israelites ate while in flight from Egypt (Deuteronomy 10:3). And he muses, "Strange are the uses of adversity."[6] The disaster of a destroyed church occasions this emotional communion with his father.

Robinson has Ames return to this memory three more times in the novel. "I remember it as if he broke the bread and put a bit of it in my mouth, though I know he didn't."[7] His memory is reframing the long-ago event into a sacramental Communion. Yet later, Ames recalls "that biscuit ashy from my father's charred hand. It all means more than I can tell you."[8] Experiences of enchantment captivate and open meanings we cannot fully fathom.

As the novel ends, Robinson has Ames meditating on this broken world. One last time the aging minister summons the imagery of ash and "the grey ember of Creation" as he reflects: "It has seemed to me sometimes as though the Lord breathes on this poor grey ember of Creation and it turns to radiance—for a moment or a year or the span of a life. And then it sinks back into itself again, and to look at it no one would know it had anything to do with fire, or light."[9] Creation glows, both with a radiance that emits light and warmth, and with the reminder that this "poor grey ember" will soon end in a cooler, ashen condition.

The Sensual as Portal to the Spiritual

"O Taste and see the goodness of the Lord" (Psalm 34:8 NRSV). The ancient Jews tuned all their senses to an appreciation of their God. In the most erotic book of the Bible, *The Song of Songs*, every part of the human body— breasts and thighs, eyes and even navels—proclaimed the glory of God. "His body is ivory work, encrusted with sapphires. His legs are alabaster columns. . . . His speech is most sweet, and he is altogether desirable" (5:12–16).

In the Catholic imagination that grew out of this tradition, the sacraments of blessing and healing were expressed through the sensual media of water and oil. In his encyclical *Laudato Si'*, Pope Francis recalls the sensual dimensions of the sacraments: "The Sacraments are a privileged way in which nature is taken up by God to become a means of mediating supernatural life. . . . Water, oil, fire and colors are taken up in all their symbolic power and incorporated in our act of praise."[10]

We have seen Christian novelists reaffirming the vital links between the sensual and the spiritual. In Mary Gordon's *Final Payments*, Isabel's experience of the sensual washing of feet on Holy Thursday and kissing the cross on Good Friday trigger in her visceral memories of bathing her crippled father, a delicate, sensual caring for flesh. Memories flood back of the everyday touching, shaving, holding of her father. These sensual memories nourished her and assisted the healing of her relationship with her father.

In Marilynne Robinson's novels, the sensual and sacramental share a similar familiarity. In *Housekeeping*, a mother relishes sensual memories of her children. These memories "filled her with a strange elation, the same pleasure she had felt when any one of them, as a sucking child, had fastened her eyes on her face and reached for her other breast, her hair, her lips, hungry to touch, eager to be filled for a while and sleep."[11] John Caputo could be commenting on Robinson's novel when he describes the kingdom of God as the everyday acts of care: "Housekeeping, cooking and cleaning, tending to the needs of the body, animal needs, the needs of the flesh, the most quotidian affairs of mundane life are not means to an end." Rather, "These works *are* the kingdom of God here on earth."[12]

Another Catholic novelist makes yet more explicit the sensual nature of the spiritual life. In *Mariette in Ecstasy*, Ron Hansen creates a story of a young woman who joins the convent of the Sisters of the Crucifixion in upstate New York. The novel blends the themes of religious life as ascetical and celibate along with the sensual nature of this spiritual life. Sister Mariette undergoes an ecstatic experience of union with Christ (that may or may not be genuine) that has erotic undertones. In the novel's title, "ecstasy" is meant to recall Bernini's famous sculpture of The Ecstasy of St. Teresa—an enchantment both spiritual and erotic. In his descriptions of the colors, sounds, and smells of the convent, Hansen combines the spiritual—the ascetic life in the convent—with the sensual. Readers meet repeated descriptions of sensual details: "tallow candles in red glass jars shudder on a high altar."[13] A nun who cares for the cattle at the convent walks alongside them, "her hands riding their caramel hides. She smells her palms and smiles."[14] When Marietta is cleaning the kitchen floor, "she is barefoot and her skirt is pinned up as high as her thigh in order to protect the habit's cloth from stain."[15] In this novel, spiritual and sensual enjoy a familiar company.

For Catholics, the sensual as portal to the spiritual finds its richest expression in lovemaking. Writing at midcentury, Graham Greene caught this belief. In *The End of the Affair*, Sarah writes in her journal—a prayer to God—about her love for Bendrix. "Could I have touched You if I hadn't touched him first, touched him as I never touched [her husband] Henry, anybody?"[16] She realizes she has been led to God through human love, even an adulterous affair.

In her memoir *The Long Loneliness*, Dorothy Day described her affection for her lover as the pathway to love of God. "I have always felt that it was life with him that brought me natural happiness, that brought me to God." She reflects, "I could not see that love between man and woman was incompatible with love of God."[17]

In Marilynne Robinson's *Gilead*, the old minister reflects on his love for his young wife—a reflection that serves as a good summary of these novelists' fusion of the sensual and the sacred. He admits to himself that he is comparing "love of God with mortal love. But I just can't see them as separate things at all. If we can be divinely fed with a morsel and divinely blessed with a touch, then the terrible pleasure we find in a particular face can certainly instruct us in the nature of the grandest love."[18]

What Does Happiness Have to Do with Christian Faith?

In the Catholic imagination, happiness has long been associated with blessing, a gift bestowed and shared, rather than private enjoyment. In the New Testament accounts of Jesus's Sermon on the Mount, the Greek term *makarios* designates both happiness and blessing: "blessed are those; happy are those." In the biblical tradition, to count one's blessings is to trace the mysterious route of authentic happiness. We are happy *because* we have received God's blessing.

But early in the Christian tradition, happiness seemed to earn a suspect reputation. Troubled by guilt and grief,

St. Augustine was profoundly impressed with the debilitating force of original sin. He judged that all humans are scarred with this universal guilt and thus deserve whatever distress comes their way—both in this life and the next. Suffering, rather than happiness, is our common lot. All current distress must be borne, in the hope of the happiness that awaits us after death.

Eight hundred years later, Thomas Aquinas had access to the recently discovered philosophy of Aristotle and this Greek's conviction about the possibility of human flourishing. Aristotle argued that flourishing—*eudaimonia* in Greek—was built into human nature. Aquinas, following Aristotle, would develop a much more positive theology that sought to incorporate the capacity to flourish along with a healthy pursuit of happiness.

We have met the puzzle of happiness in Evelyn Waugh's *Brideshead Revisited* when Sebastian, distressed by his own eccentric Catholic family, wonders, "I wouldn't know which of them was happy. Anyway, however you look at it, happiness doesn't seem to have much to do with it."[19]

In Gordon's *Final Payments*, Isabel's father opines that "one did not look for happiness on earth; there was a glory in poverty."[20] In *The Company of Women*, Father Cyprian tries to convince Felicitas, "We were not put on earth to be happy"[21] but, as the catechism says, to know, love and serve God. In the final section of the novel, Father Cyprian comes to realize that he has been "pulled down by the irresistible gravity of affection and regard" of these women and especially the young Felicitas. "I have had to learn ordinary happiness, and from ordinary happiness, the first real peace of my life." Despite his disappointment about what he has accomplished as a priest, he admits, "It is true, I am happier than I have ever been."[22]

Dorothy Day, as early as 1949, confessed, "We want to be happy, we want others to be happy, we want to see some of this joy of life which children have, we want to see people intoxicated with God, or just filled with the good steady joy of knowing that Christ is King."[23] In her memoir *The Long Loneliness*, she makes the most explicit linking of natural happiness and love of God. Reflecting on her lover Forster Batterham, she writes, "I have always felt that it was life that brought me natural happiness, that brought me to God."[24]

The return of enchantment arrives with the embrace of happiness as companion of grace.

What Does Beauty Have to Do with Christian Faith?

One thing I ask of the Lord, that will I seek after: to live in the house of the Lord all the days of my life, to behold the beauty of the Lord. (Psalms 27)

A puzzle that runs through the Catholic imagination concerns the place of beauty in the Christian story. Do the beautiful things in the world recruit our affection, lifting our sight to the Source of all loveliness? Or does beauty serve more regularly to seduce and distract us from our higher, more austere calling? Has the disenchantment of the modern world so darkened the luster of the beautiful that its sacramental power to enchant has been compromised or even erased?

Many Christians have been tutored in Augustine's suspicion of human beauty. Calvin, strongly influenced by Augustine, spoke of human nature as totally corrupt. If our lives are utterly distorted by original sin, we are likely to be led astray by the beauty we meet in life. Augustine realized that, in loving God, he did "love a kind of light, melody, fragrance, food, touch when I love my God."[25] But he was especially wary of "glowing and beautiful colors. These things must not take hold of my soul; that is for God to do."[26]

Troubled by the allure of beauty, Augustine proposed a spiritual strategy to keep earthly and divine delights distinct. In his definition, *enjoyment* would mean the utter surrender of one's heart to what is being relished; he thus proposed that we may enjoy only God. All else in creation is only to be used, not enjoyed. "We must use this world, not enjoy it."[27] All that is not God—that is, every lovely part of creation—can only be appreciated as an instrument to lead us to God.

In the Catholic novels we have considered, we see this tension on display. In *Brideshead Revisited*, Evelyn Waugh cannot conceal his suspicion of beauty: we learn that Sebastian "was magically beautiful, with that epicene quality which in extreme youth sings loud for love and withers at the first cold wind." Sebastian's sister Julia had grown into a "haunting, magical sadness which spoke straight to the heart and struck silence; it was the completion of her beauty."[28] Fragile, human beauty is likely to soon "wither" or culminate in a shroud of sadness.

The stories of Flannery O'Connor have little room for beauty. Her vocational focus was on

the disfigured; "We're all grotesque."[29] In her stories Grace is remedial, wrenching souls away from
their inbuilt perversities. Perhaps the one excep-
tion is her vision of a motley crew of humans
ascending toward the heavens in her rendition of
the Communion of Saints; this portrait has its own
earthy enchantment.

Despite the caution about beauty we have met in
many of these novels, Christian art, liturgy and archi-
tecture have always been devoted to beauty. Beautiful statues of saints, sacred music, and the sumptuous
colors and pungent incense of Catholic rituals are
meant to arouse us to worship of our Creator. They
are meant to charm us and grace our lives. *Jubilee*
magazine, in articles and photos that are contemporary with O'Connor's short stories, conveyed great
enthusiasm for the new church art that was beginning to emerge. Many readers disapproved of these
new ventures, their disapproval registered in letters to
the editor.

With the return of enchantment in the second half
of the century, we saw a new enthusiasm for natural
beauty, a beauty that continually re-enchants our
world that has been disfigured by violence. Both
Mary Gordon and Marilynne Robinson hold up
the beauty of the sensual as portal to the sacred.
Everyday life, with its regular contact with water,
light, and generous touch, provides us with rituals of the ordinary and experiences of the world's
sacramental charm.

Laughter and Grace

God has done great things for us; our mouth is filled with
laughter and our tongue with shouts of joy. (Psalm 126)

Laughter, like happiness, serves as currency in the Beat-itudes: "Blessed are you who weep now, for you will laugh" (Luke 6:21). Laughter is a fitting response to the marvels God has done for us. The first sound of laugh-ter in the Bible arises when Abraham and Sarah both chuckle at the thought of having a child in their old age (Genesis 18:11–12). This was a laugh not of delight but incredulity, but laughter nonetheless as a response to God's startling revelation.

Drama critic John Lahr describes the healing force of laughter: "When we say laughter lifts our spirits, we mean it works as a sort of stage-managed resurrection—we are somehow taken out of ourselves . . . and in that instant, life becomes luminous again."[30] Here again, art and religion ("resurrection") promote experiences of enchantment.

Early in the Catholic tradition, believers lost their enthusiasm for laughter. Their faith, centered on a cru-cified Lord, was not a laughing matter. Philosopher Richard Sorabji judges that "the predominant attitude to laughter in much of ancient philosophy, and still more in the Church Fathers, was disapproval."[31] This was graphically the case with St. Augustine; in his memoir *Confessions*, he remembers the laughter that arose at his own expense: laughter as ridicule and derision.

In *The Company of Women*, Gordon highlights two very different kinds of laughter. As Father Cyprian and his farmer friend "teach" Felicitas about the noxious odors of animal excrement, their laughter sears Felicitas's soul. Humiliated, "Felicitas would always remember that laugh. In that laugh she was the other, she would know always in that laugh what it was to be the outsider." And for years to come she "vowed never to forgive the force, the laughter."[32]

But by the conclusion of *Final Payments*, Isabel has learned the laughter of delight and companionship. In a final scene, her women friends laugh at her atrocious haircut (residue of an earlier piety), but their laughter enfolds and enheartens Isabel. "And our laughter was solid."[33]

Gordon's *The Company of Women* concludes on the same note, but with greater emphasis. As Felicitas reconciles with her mother and Father Cyprian, she observes, "I began noticing things in the world that made me laugh." This ability to laugh is not far from enchantment. As she reconciled with Father Cyprian, they both rediscovered laughter: now "we laughed as we hadn't laughed in years. We got back what we were both afraid we had lost forever: our great pleasure in each other."[34]

In *Gilead*, Marilynne Robinson provides us the richest expression about laughter and its potential. The old preacher John Ames wonders at the sheer beauty of people breaking into laughter. As he watched two young men joking around, he mused, "It is an amazing thing to watch people laugh, the way it sort of takes them over . . . so I wonder what it is and where it comes from, and I wonder what it expends out of your system, so that you have to do it till you're done." And he adds, "At that point I began to suspect, as I have from time to time, that grace has a grand laughter in it."[35] For this old man, laughter measures the enchanting presence of grace.

"The Christian of the future will be a mystic or will not exist at all."

The great Catholic theologian Karl Rahner, writing in 1971, departed from his typically complex theologizing to offer this startling suggestion. What could he mean by this radical claim? In an essay, "Christian Living Formerly and Today," he wrote of "a mysticism of daily life, the finding of God in all things."[36] This Jesuit orientation, begun in the spirituality of Ignatius Loyola, argued that at the heart of the Catholic imagination lay a mystical or enchanted vision of God's presence throughout creation. Rahner could have been thinking of the poetry of another Jesuit, Gerard Manley Hopkins: "The world is charged with the grandeur of God."

Rahner was seeking to rescue an appreciation of "mystic" from its exotic nuances. Mysticism had come to occupy a niche in Christian life, like that of "saint," that placed it beyond the experience of ordinary believers. Three decades before Rahner's remark, fellow Jesuit Pierre Teilhard de Chardin had given a compelling example of what a more ordinary mysticism might look like.

In 1915, Teilhard found himself ministering to French soldiers in the Great War. He found that when there was no church in which to offer Mass, he would celebrate the Eucharist without chalice and vestments that traditionally accompanied this sacramental prayer. He called this his "Mass on the world."[37]

With the end of the war, Teilhard returned to his career as scientist, participating in various expeditions in northern China and Mongolia. Here, too, he would find himself on an excavation dig without an opportunity to offer Mass in the traditional fashion. He again would celebrate the Eucharist as a "Mass on the world." He eventually composed a prayer for such occasions. "Since once again, Lord . . . I have neither bread, nor wine, nor altar, I will raise myself beyond these symbols, up to the pure majesty of the real itself; I, your priest, will make the whole earth my altar and on it will offer to you all the labours and sufferings of the world."[38]

As the sun rises on an excavation site in Asia, he asks God to "grant me the remembrance and the mystic presence of all those whom the light is now awakening to the new day." He prays, "One by one, Lord, I see and love all those whom you have given me to sustain and charm my life."[39] And beyond this group of friends and colleagues, he conjures in his imagination "this restless multitude, confused or orderly, the immensity of which terrifies us; this ocean of humanity."[40] We hear here the theme near the heart of the Catholic imagination: the Communion of Saints.

The "Mass of the world" now reaches its climax: "Through the consecration of the world the luminosity and fragrance which suffuse the universe take on for me the lineaments of a body and a face—you."[41] At the heart of the Eucharist, and at the core of the Catholic imagination, is the transfiguration of the earthly bread and wine into the Body of Christ. Teilhard extends this enchantment to include the entire material world now transfigured as God's own body.

Teilhard's mystical faith testifies to a sacramental vision of God's presence within every aspect of creation. His "Mass on the world" reminds us that the essence of the Eucharist is not in the chalice, paten, proper vestments or even the Latin words of consecration, but in the consecration of every part of the world into the dazzling unfolding of a universal salvation. Rahner's remark suggests that without some sense of this enchantment, future Christians will find it difficult to live a life of robust faith.

In the biblical story that begins in a garden, other enchantments ensue: a burning bush that captivates Moses; an angel announcing seemingly impossible events to Mary; Jesus, after his death, appearing to his friends very much like a ghost. We are entranced by gospel parables; we are captivated by the lives of saints. The mystery that runs through all these events is not discouraging, but bracing. It fits the elusiveness of our own lives.

Having abandoned belief in literal magic, we are able to describe a theatrical drama as magical. No longer believing in spells, we can picture a charming novel as spellbinding. When we no long adhere to ancient beliefs about ghosts, we are willing to entertain John Lahr's question, "Can we agree that we're all haunted? The ghost world is part of our world. We carry within us the good and the bad, the spoken and unspoken imperatives of our missing loved ones."[42] Literary critic Dan Chiasson writes that "metaphor is a poet's spell, her magic; more than any other feature of poetry, it transforms reality."[43] But metaphor is also what animates the sacred scriptures and the religious rituals in which the enchantments of God's grace are registered and celebrated.

Mary Gordon, Annie Dillard, Pope Francis, and Marilynne Robinson all witness to the belief that creation is teeming with enchantment. The world's water, light, and laughter are already sacramental, long before religious rituals name them so. Disenchantment does describe the world for many souls, casting a pall over everyday life. Yet others glimpse, at least on occasion, what Dillard so dramatically insisted: "The whole show has been on fire from the word go."[44] Robinson's novels return again and again to the belief in this enchantment: "Wherever you turn your eyes the world can shine like transfiguration."[45]

[1]   Evelyn Waugh, *Brideshead Revisited*, 31.
[2]   Thomas Merton, *The Seven Storey Mountain*, 410.
[3]   Tessa Hadley, "At Home in the Past," *The New Yorker*, 75.
[4]   Marilynne Robinson, *Housekeeeping*, 192.
[5]   Robinson, 152.
[6]   Robinson, *Gilead*, 95
[7]   Robinson, 102
[8]   Robinson, 114.
[9]   Robinson, 245.
[10]   *Laudato Si'*, no. 235.
[11]   Robinson, *Housekeeping*, 11.
[12]   John Caputo, *Hoping against Hope*, 83.
[13]   Ron Hansen, *Mariette in Ecstasy*, 5.
[14]   Hansen, 55.
[15]   Hansen, 62.
[16]   Graham Greene, *The End of the Affair*, 123.
[17]   Dorothy Day, *The Long Loneliness*, 135.
[18]   Robinson, *Gilead*, 204.
[19]   Waugh, *Brideshead Revisited*, 89.
[20]   Gordon, *Final Payments*, 4
[21]   Gordon, *The Company of Women*, 82
[22]   Gordon, 284, 287.
[23]   Dorothy Day, *Selected Writings*, 102.
[24]   Day, *The Long Loneliness*, 134.
[25]   Augustine, *Confessions*, 10.6.
[26]   Augustine, 10.34.
[27]   John Mahoney, *The Making of Moral Theology*, 44.
[28]   Waugh, 31.
[29]   O'Connor, *Mystery and Manners*, 233.
[30]   John Lahr, "The Laughing Cure," *The New Yorker*, 211.
[31]   Richard Sorabji, *Emotions and Peace of Mind*, 390.
[32]   Gordon, *The Company of Women*, 44.
[33]   Gordon, *Final Payments*, 297.
[34]   Gordon, *The Company of Women*, 255.
[35]   Robinson, *Gilead*, 207.
[36]   Karl Rahner, "Mystical Experience and Mystical Theology," *Theological Investigations*, 94.
[37]   Thomas King, *Teilhard's Mass*, 145.
[38]   King.
[39]   King.
[40]   King, 146.
[41]   King, 149.
[42]   Lahr, "Trapped in Time," 92.
[43]   Dan Chiasson, "Jana Prikryl's 'The After Party,'" *The New Yorker*, 76.
[44]   Annie Dillard, *Pilgrim at Tinker Creek*, 11.
[45]   Robinson, *Gilead*, 245.

BIBLIOGRAPHY

Ackroyd, Peter. *T. S. Eliot: A Life*. New York: Simon and Schuster, 1984.

Anderson, Benedict. *Imagined Communities*. London: Verso, 1983.

Augustine. *Confessions of St. Augustine,* Garden City, NY: Doubleday, 1960.

Bardugo, Leigh. "Alice Hoffman's 'Nightbird.'" *The New York Times Sunday Book Review*, April 12, 2015. https://www.nytimes.com/2015/04/12/books/review/alice-hoffmans-nightbird.html.

Bernanos, George. *The Diary of a Country Priest*. New York: Macmillan, 1937.

Berry, Wendell. "An Entrance to the Woods." *The Art of the Personal Essay: An Anthology from the Classical Era to the Present*. Selected and with an introduction by Phillip Lopate, 671–79. New York: Anchor, 1996.

Bettelheim, Bruno. *The Uses of Enchantment: The Meaning and Importance of Fairy Tales*. New York: Knopf, 1976.

Bottum, Joseph. "The Things We Share: A Catholic's Case for Same-Sex Marriage." *Commonweal*, August 23, 2013. https://www.commonwealmagazine.org/things-we-share.

Brooks, David. "The Devotional Leap." *The New York Times*, January 23, 2015.

Buckley, William F., Jr. *God and Man at Yale: The Superstitions of "Academic Freedom."* Washington, DC: Regnery, 1951.

Burgess, Anthony. *Here Comes Everybody: An Introduction to James Joyce for the Ordinary Reader*. London: Faber and Faber, 1965.

Bynum, Caroline Walker. *Metamorphosis and Identity.* Cambridge, MA: MIT Press, 2001.

Caputo, John. *Hoping against Hope.* Minneapolis, MN: Fortress, 2015.

Chardin, Teilhard de. *The Divine Milieu.* New York: Harper & Row, 1960.

———. *The Phenomenon of Man.* New York: Harper & Row, 1959.

Chesterton, G. K. *The Complete Father Brown Stories of G. K. Chesterton.* London: Wordsworth Classics, 1992.

Chiasson, Dan. "Jana Prikryl's 'The After Party.'" *The New Yorker*, August 8 & 15, 2016: 75–77.

Congar, Yves. "The Layman, the Church, and the World." *Jubilee*, June 1957: 16–19.

Connelly, William. *A World of Becoming.* Durham, NC: Duke University Press, 2011.

Daston, Lorraine J. and Katharine Park. *Wonders and the Order of Nature, 1150–1750.* New York: Zone, 1998.

Day, Dorothy. *Dorothy Day: Selected Writings.* Edited by Robert Ellberg. New York: Orbis Books, 1983.

———. *The Long Loneliness.* San Francisco, CA: Harper & Row, 1952.

Dillard, Annie. *Pilgrim at Tinker Creek.* New York: HarperCollins, 1974.

———. *The Abundance.* San Francisco, CA: Ecco/HarperCollins, 2016.

Dupré, Louis. *Passage to Modernity: An Essay in the Hermeneutics of Nature and Culture.* New Haven: Yale University Press, 1993.

Dupuy, Edward. "The 4 p.m. Blues." *Commonweal*, December 15, 2015: 31–33.

Egan, Harvey. "The Mystical Theology of Karl Rahner." *The Way*, 52 (2013): 43–62.

Elie, Paul. *The Life You Save May Be Your Own: An American Pilgrimage*. New York: Farrar, Straus and Giroux, 2003.

Eliot, T. S. *The Waste Land*. New York: Norton, 2001.

———. "Ash Wednesday." In *T. S. Eliot, The Waste Land and Other Poems*. Selected and with an introduction by Helen Vendler. New York: Penguin, 1998.

———. *Four Quartets*. Orlando, FL: Harcourt, 1943.

———. *The Idea of a Christian Society*. London: Faber and Faber, 1939.

———. *On Poetry and Poets*. New York: Farrar, Straus and Giroux. 1943.

Ellmann, Richard. *James Joyce*. New York: Oxford University Press, New and Revised Edition, 1982.

Evans, Joseph and Leo Ward, eds. *The Social and Political Philosophy of Jacques Maritain: Selected Readings*. Notre Dame, IN: University of Notre Dame, 1955.

Forest, Jim. *All is Grace: A Biography of Dorothy Day*. New York: Orbis Books, 2011.

Francis. *Laudato Si'*. Huntington, IN: Our Sunday Visitor, 2015.

Fuller, Robert. *Wonder: From Emotion to Spirituality*. Chapel Hill: University of North Carolina Press, 2006.

Gooch, Brad. *Flannery: A Life of Flannery O'Connor*. New York: Little, Brown, 2009.

Gordon, Mary. *Final Payments*. New York: Random House, 1978.

———. *The Company of Women*. New York: Ballantine, 1980.

———. "Getting Here from There: A Writer's Reflections on a Religious Past." In *Good Boys and Dead Girls and Other Essays*, 166. New York: Penguin, 1992.

Greeley, Andrew. *The Catholic Imagination*. Berkeley: University of California Press, 2001.

Greene, Graham. *The End of the Affair*. New York: Penguin, 1951.

———. *The Power and the Glory*. New York: Penguin, 1940.

———. *The Heart of the Matter*. New York: Viking Press, 1948.

Greene, Richard, ed. *Graham Greene: A Life in Letters*. New York: Norton, 2008.

Guardini, Romano. "The Patience of God." *Jubilee*, May 1957: 16–19.

Hadley, Tessa. "At Home in the Past," *The New Yorker*, June 6 & 13, 2016: 75–77.

Haidt, Jonathan. *The Happiness Hypothesis*. New York: Basic Books, 2006.

Hansen, Ron. *Mariette in Ecstasy*. New York: HarperCollins, 1991.

Hilkert, Catherine. *Naming Grace*. New York: Continuum, 1997.

Hopkins, Gerard Manley. *Gerard Manley Hopkins: The Major Works*. Edited by Catherine Philips. New York: Oxford University Press, 1986.

Hynes, Samuel, ed. *Graham Greene: A Collection of Critical Essays*. Englewood Cliffs, NJ: Prentice-Hall, 1973.

Isaacson, Walter. "Walker Percy's Theory of Hurricanes." *The New York Times Sunday Book Review*, August 4, 2015. https://www.nytimes.com/2015/08/09/books/review/walker-percys-theory-of-hurricanes.html.

Johnson, Diane. "Moral of the Story." *The New York Times*, October 5, 2014.

Johnson, Elizabeth. *Friends of God and Prophets: A Feminist Theological Reading of the Communion of Saints*. New York: Continuum, 1998.

Joyce, James. *A Portrait of the Artist as a Young Man*. New York: Penguin, 2003.

———. *Dubliners*. New York: Bantam Classic, 2005.

———. *Ulysses*. New York: Vintage Books, 1986.

Keltner, Dacher. *Born to be Good*. New York: Norton, 2009.

Keltner, Dacher and Jonathan Haidt. "Approaching Awe, a Moral, Spiritual and Aesthetic Emotion," *Cognition and Emotion*, 17, no. 2 (2003): 297–314.

Ker, Ian. *The Catholic Revival in English Literature, 1845–61*. Notre Dame, IN: University of Notre Dame Press, 2003.

King, Thomas. *Teilhard's Mass: Approaches to "The Mass on the World."* New York: Paulist Press, 2005.

Lahr, John. "Trapped in Time: '*Mary Rose,*' and '*Salvage.*'" *The New Yorker*. March 5, 2007: 92–93.

———. "The Laughing Cure." *The New Yorker*, October 18, 2004: 211–212.

Lamott, Anne. *Small Victories*. New York: Riverhead Books, 2014.

Mahoney, John. *The Making of Moral Theology*. Oxford: Clarendon Press, 1987.

Maritain, Jacques. *True Humanism*. New York: Scribner, 1938.

———. *Art and Scholasticism*. Translated by J. E. Scanlan. New York: Scribner, 1947.

———. *The Range of Reason*. New York: Scribner, 1952.

———. *Reflections on America*. New York: Scribner, 1958.

———. "The Christian and History." *Jubilee*. November 1957: 37–40.

Mauriac, François. *Viper's Tangle*. New York: Sheed & Ward, 1933.

McCarty, Doran. *Teilhard de Chardin.* Waco, TX: Word Books, 1976.

McGregor, Michael. *Pure Act: The Uncommon Life of Robert Lax.* New York: Fordham University Press, 2015.

McInerny, Ralph. *Some Catholic Writers.* South Bend, IN: St. Augustine's Press, 2007.

Menand, Louis. "Adam Begley's 'Updike,'" *The New Yorker,* April 28, 2014: 70–76.

Merton, Thomas. *The Seven Storey Mountain.* New York: Harcourt, 1948.

———. *In The Dark Before Dawn: New Selected Poems of Thomas Merton.* Edited by Lynn Szabo. Preface by Kathleen Norris. New York: New Directions, 2005.

———. *Seeds of Contemplation.* Norfolk, CT: J. Laughlin, 1949.

———. "The Second Coming," *Jubilee,* April 1956: 6–9.

Norman, Sherry. *The Life of Graham Greene, vol. 1, 1904–1939.* Harmondsworth, England: Penguin, 1990.

Nussbaum, Martha. *Cultivating Humanity.* Cambridge, MA: Harvard University Press, 1997.

Acocella, Joan. "Lonesome Road." *The New Yorker,* October 6, 2014: 79–82.

O'Connor, Flannery. *The Complete Stories.* New York: Farrar, Straus and Giroux, 1989.

———. *Mystery and Manners: Occasional Prose.* Edited by Sally and Robert Fitzgerald. New York: Farrar, Straus and Giroux, 1969.

———. *The Habit of Being: Letters of Flannery O'Connor.* Edited with an introduction by Sally Fitzgerald. New York: Farrar, Straus and Giroux, 1979.

Paul VI. *Pastoral Constitution on the Church in the Modern World (Gaudium et Spes).* Boston: Pauline Books and Media, 1966.

Percy, Walker. *The Moviegoer*. New York: Random House, 1960.

———. *The Last Gentleman*. New York: Farrar, Straus and Giroux, 1966.

———. *Signposts in a Strange Land*. New York: Farrar, Straus and Giroux, 1991.

Powers, J. F. *The Presence of Grace*. New York: Atheneum, 1962 (originally published in 1956).

Rahner, Karl. "Mystical Experience and Mystical Theology." *Theological Investigations*, volume 17, 90–99. Translated by Margaret Kohl. New York: Crossroad, 1981.

Ricoeur, Paul. *The Symbolism of Evil*. Boston: Beacon Press, 1963.

Rivera, Mary Anne. "Jubilee: A Magazine of the Church and her People: Toward a Vatican II Ecclesiology." *Logos: A Journal of Catholic Thought and Culture*, September 22, 2007: 77–103.

Robinson, Marilynne. *Housekeeping*. New York: Farrar, Straus and Giroux, 1980.

———. *Gilead*. New York: Farrar, Straus and Giroux, 2004.

———. *Home*. New York: Farrar, Straus and Giroux, 2008.

———. *When I Was a Child I Read Books*. New York: Farrar, Straus and Giroux, 2012.

———. *Lila*. New York: Farrar, Straus and Giroux, 2014.

———. *The Givenness of Things*. New York: Farrar, Straus and Giroux. 2015.

Samway, Patrick. *Walker Percy: A Life*. Chicago: Loyola Press, 1997.

Scarry, Elaine. *On Beauty and Being Just*. NJ: Princeton University Press, 1999.

Schjeldahl, Peter. "El Greco at the Met." *The New Yorker*, October 20, 2003: 198–99.

Schönborn, Christoph Cardinal. *Chance or Purpose? Creation, Evolution, and a Rational Faith*. New York: Ignatius Press, 2007.

Sheed, Wilfrid. "Catholics and the Pill: A Review of John Rock's *The Time has Come*," *Jubilee*, July 1963.

Sorabji, Richard. *Emotions and Peace of Mind: From Stoic Agitation to Christian Temptation*. New York: Oxford University Press, 2000.

Steiner, George. *Real Presences*. Chicago: University of Chicago Press, 1989.

Sullivan, Oona. "Also of Interest," *Jubilee*, August 1960: 44–46.

Sykes, Christopher. *Evelyn Waugh: A Biography*. London: Collins, 1975.

Tavard, George. "The Eucharist," *Jubilee*, June 1960: 8–11.

Taylor, Charles. *A Secular Age*. Cambridge, MA: Harvard University Press, 2007.

———. "Disenchantment-Reenchantment." In *Dilemmas and Connections*, 287–302. Cambridge, MA: Harvard University Press, 2011.

Tracy, David. *The Analogical Imagination*. New York: Crossroad, 1981.

Traina, Cristina. *Erotic Attunement: Parenthood and the Ethics of Sensuality between Unequals*. Chicago: University of Chicago Press, 2011.

Unger, Roberto. *Passion: An Essay on Personality*. New York: The Free Press, 1984.

Vatican II. "Declaration on the Relation of the Church to Non-Christian Religions *Nostra Aetate*." In *Vatican II: Constitutions, Decrees and Declarations*, 569–74. Edited by Austin Flannery, O.P., Northport, NY: Costello Publishing, 1996.

Volk, Tyler. *Gaia's Body: Toward a Physiology of Earth*. New York: Copernicus, 1997.

Waugh, Evelyn. *Brideshead Revisited*. New York: Little, Brown and Company, 1945.

———. *Sword of Honor*. New York: Back Bay Books, 1966.

Weems, Scott. *Ha: The Science of When We Laugh and Why*. New York: Basic Books, 2014.

Whitehead, James and Evelyn. *Nourishing the Spirit: The Healing Emotions of Wonder, Joy, Compassion and Hope*. Maryknoll, NY: Orbis Books, 2012.

Wills, Garry. *The Future of the Catholic Church with Pope Francis*. New York: Viking, 2015.

Wilson, Edward O. *Consilience: The Unity of Knowledge*. New York: Knopf, 1998.

Wiman, Christian. *My Bright Abyss: Meditations of a Modern Believer*. New York: Farrar, Straus and Giroux, 2013.

Wolfe, Gregory. *Beauty Will Save the World: Recovering the Human in an Ideological Age*. Wilmington, DE: Intercollegiate Studies Institute, 2011.

Index

About the Authors

Evelyn Eaton Whitehead is a developmental psychologist (PhD, University of Chicago) and James Whitehead is a Catholic theologian and historian of religion (PhD, Harvard University). Married since 1970, the Whiteheads have served on the theology faculty at Notre Dame University and for forty-five years as professors at the Institute of Pastoral Studies, Loyola University, Chicago. During that time they published twenty books, a number of which have been translated into five foreign languages.

About the Publisher

The Crossroad Publishing Company publishes Crossroad and Herder & Herder books. We offer a 200-year global family tradition of books on spiritual living and religious thought. We promote reading as a time-tested discipline for focus and understanding. We help authors shape, clarify, write, and effectively promote their ideas. We select, edit, and distribute books. With our expertise and passion, we provide wholesome spiritual nourishment for heart, mind, and soul through the written word.